Prince Cl

GW01401429

Burford Delannoy

Alpha Editions

This edition published in 2024

ISBN 9789362098757

Design and Setting By

Alpha Editions

www.alphaedis.com

Email - info@alphaedis.com

Contents

CHAPTER I

HERO AND HEROINE MEET

The advent of its regatta is usually the herald of a sea-side season's demise. Wivernsea, as yet, is not sufficiently developed to justify indulgence in a water festival. So far, its carnival flights have been confined within the limits of flower shows and the treats of its Sunday school.

The builder—his surname is Jerry—is around with a rule though. His conspiracy with the man who plots lands and dispenses free luncheons and railway tickets, will possibly wreak a change on that part of the map's countenance. Increased population may render the place more famous—or infamous. So very much depends on one's viewpoint.

The houses of Wivernsea are built in its bay. Stuck in round the fringe of it like teeth in a lower jaw. Picture to yourself the long ago—the bay's origin—and the present appearance of the place may come before you. If possible to introduce a belief that there were giants in the earth in those days it will make realization simpler. Because it looks as if a mammoth had snapped at the coast just there and bitten out a huge mouthful.

If your imagination is sufficiently elastic to give play to it, conceive houses being dropped into the marks left by the giant's teeth—a sort of dental stopping. So may be garnered a fair idea of the presentment of this particular indentation in the land.

When the goose of Michaelmas is shaking in its scales, Wivernsea lodging letters encroach on the farmer's privilege. The closing time of their harvest is near enough to be grumbled at. It is painful knowledge to them that visitors scuttle away as September ends. The exodus is due to some absurd belief that the weather then—like a school at the advent of the holidays— breaks up.

In the ears of one man—William Masters by name, binder-together-of-sensational-incidents in-book-form by profession—such grumbles tingled pleasantly. Because the usual October Wivernsea weather is mild and bright and rainless. Being a non-gregarious man, the place shaped before his eyes as a land flowing with milk and honey. He knew it to be good then.

Knowledge is the wing on which we fly to heaven. In this instance, the author's flight from London was via the London and South Western Railway Company's terminus. Later on he told himself that it was proving—veritably—his Waterloo.

Wivernsea's sea wall is known locally as the Esplanade. Euphemisms—sacrifices to vanity at the expense of truth—are not uncommon objects of the seashore. The walk terminated eastwards with the abruptness of a cinematograph view. A private owner claimed the land there.

It was not an undisputed claim. Opposition made the owner handle the matter with mailed fist. To make his position stronger he erected a high wall. If it did not prevent his opponents going further with their labial opposition, it effectually prevented them from going further along the parade.

The embellishments of the wall were, apparently, the outcome of deep thought. Its top was artistically embroidered with spikes and broken bottles. This sharply jagged crown was known locally as a shivery-freeze. Give the average man an opportunity to mispronounce a word and his success may be counted on every time.

Warnings to trespassers and threats of prosecution garnished the wall's face with the liberality of almonds in a piece of French rock. The everyday man might well be excused a fear that there was danger in letting an unguarded eye rest on it.

Amongst others, the wall barred the easterly progress of William Masters. In his instance no chagrin resulted. It was a boast of his that he possessed views of his own: the things which other people smile at unpleasantly and label eccentricities. The owner of the wall was a man after his own heart. Undoubtedly a fellow-feeling makes us wondrous kind.

It is not good that man should be alone. But the author had not yet realized the greatness of that truth. He had been heard to voice the nature of his Ultima Thule: undisturbed existence in a cot. Not beside the hill, but in the centre of a big field. The situation to be enhanced by possession of a shot gun, wherewith to pepper trespassers on his solitude.

Strangers who heard Masters speak so, felt inclination to move away a pace; were prompted to thoughts of Hanwell and Colney Hatch. His friends—another boast of his was the poverty of their number—smiled. The idea of Masters hurting a fly appealed to the humour in them.

But, as the blackest hat may have a silver-paper lining, so the wall served a good purpose. It acted as a shelter from the one thing which disturbed the enjoyment of October in Wivernsea: that wind which is said to be good for neither man nor beast. Thoughtful hands had placed a comfortable seat within the wall's shelter.

Knowledge of these things had inspired Masters' journey to Wivernsea. Where he had stayed before the landlady had rooms vacant. She knew his requirements and, hitherto, had suited him admirably. Had even acquired the knowledge that his visits to Wivernsea were not prompted solely by a desire to hear her talk!

Having done justice to a hastily prepared luncheon, Masters slipped a note book into his pocket and sallied forth. His route was easterly, its termination his favourite seat at the end of the Parade. There were some hours left of warmth and sunshine: the author's intent was to avail himself of them.

Seated, he for a time succumbed to the charm of the water as it stole out and away. Listened to its lapping as it broadened the ribbon of sand at each receding wave. Then, turning a deaf ear to the charm and his eyes on to his note book, he buried himself in the particular chapter on which he was engaged.

The writer's concentration was not of the plumbless kind. Sound of a girl's voice roused him from his depth of thought. It should not be gathered from that that the sex had any extraordinary influence over him—save when it was very young.

He loved children. Loved them best before the rubbing off of what is called their corners: the sweetness of what is actually the innocence we all come into the world with—which it seems the business of the world to destroy.

Masters guessed from the voice that it belonged to a very little girl. Looking up, saw standing in front of him proof of the correctness of his guess. A blue-eyed—wide-open-eyed-with-astonishment too at seeing him there—little maid. She had turned the parade corner, and in doing so came on him unexpectedly. It was plain that she had pulled up suddenly at seeing him there. Just as suddenly called out in her clear, childish treble:

"Oh! There's someone on your seat, Miss Mivvins!"

The young lady so addressed came into view at that moment, round the bushes planted at the corner—the little one having, as usual, run on ahead.

Miss Mivvins flushed a little. Becomingly, for otherwise the face might have been considered a trifle too pale. The possibility of the child's speech being considered rude induced her to say in an undertone:

"Hush, Gracie, dear!"

The speech reached Masters' ears. He was at once struck with the governess's singularly sweet voice. When he looked at the place whence the voice issued, he thought it the prettiest mouth he had ever set eyes on. The little droop of sadness at its corners mellowed rather than took away from the sweetness of it.

The lips—ripe red in colour, Cupid's bowed in shape—enchanting as they were, did not hold his attention in iron bonds. His glance wandered to her eyes and hair. From that inspection was formed an opinion—one which he never changed.

The features were the most beautiful and womanly ones he had ever seen. Just as sweet a face as a woman with golden hair—that peculiar tint of gold which the sun ever seems anxious to search amongst—and forget-me-not eyes, can possess at the age of three-and twenty. She was good to look upon.

Observation was a trick of Masters' trade. The practice of it enabled him to paint a picture in a paragraph. What he saw in one glimpse of Miss Mivvins' face was eloquence itself. But of that gentle, outward-going radiance in her eyes the merest layman would have been sentient. It was the kind of which one felt even a blind man must be conscious.

Details appealed to Masters just then. He happened to be engaged at the moment on the description of a heroine. When he saw Miss Mivvins his difficulty about shaping the book-woman vanished. In flesh and blood she stood before him. All he needed was to describe what he saw: she would fit in all respects.

Save her name. He was not particularly struck with that.

CHAPTER II

THE CHILD, THE WISE MAN, AND THE LADY

Proverbially women love men's approbation. Something of the feeling within him must have evidenced itself in Masters' eyes. His attentive scrutiny—despite all there was of respect in it—did not, apparently, please Miss Mivvins. Possibly, she was inclined to consider his admiration rudeness. Anyway she called:

"Come, Gracie!"

Taking the child's little hand in her own neatly gloved one as she spoke, the woman turned, evidently intent on walking back in the direction whence she had come.

That brought Masters to his feet in a moment—cap in hand, and apology in mouth. Full of crudities as was his character, he possessed an instinctive courtesy. In all the arraignments for his breaches of Society's unwritten laws, impoliteness had never figured. He spoke; said:

"Pray do not let me drive you away! Possession may be nine points of the law, but we may consider ourselves beyond the pale of its practice here. If, as I hear—from lips the truth of which it would be absurd to doubt—that this is considered your seat," his smile was not an unpleasing one, "I should never forgive myself if trespass of mine interfered with the owner's use of it."

"Is that pen you are using," inquired Gracie suddenly, à propos of nothing, "one of those you put the ink in at the wrong end, and trickle it out of the other?"

A softness blended with the smile on Masters' face and merged into that kindly expression of the strong for the weak. It was the successful catching of just such tenderness which made Landseer's name figure so prominently in the world of Art. As the author looked down at the mite from his six-feet altitude, the look on his face was an irresistible reminder of a St. Bernard's kindness to a toy terrier.

"You have accurately described it, little woman," he answered. "But it does not always trickle when you want it to—though it generally does when you don't."

The child looked mystified; evidently deemed further explanation necessary. Miss Mivvins was still standing, waiting to go. Masters hesitated; looked from one to the other. Politeness made him say:

"I am leaving—pray be seated."

But the woman saw through that. Would have been very high up the fool grade indeed had she failed to do so. It really was quite too transparent an artifice. When truth is sacrificed on the altar of politeness the ceremony needs skill, otherwise the lie becomes even more offensive than the act it was to cover.

His little speech induced her to take a step forward; made her say:

"Oh, no! Do not let me drive you away!"

She spoke impulsively; hurriedly. Masters thought with everything in the tone that was desirable in a woman's voice. He smiled as he expostulated:

"But you remember, surely—it is not many moments ago—you were quite willing to allow me to drive you away."

Then she smiled too. Smiles which brought into play mouth and eyes and the dimples in her cheeks. From his own face the gravity—some people called it Austerity—had already departed. There was a peculiarly softening influence about Miss Mivvins. Perhaps his own relaxing was the result of that.

"It is a long seat."

He indicated its measurement with a sweep of his hand as he spoke; continued:

"Let its length be our way out of the difficulty—it is a long lane that has no turning. How will it be if we make it large enough for both?"

It was a tentative sort of invitation. An invisible olive branch to which her hand went out. Again she smiled. A moment's hesitation ... then seated herself.

From the bag depending by silken cords from her wrist she drew a book. Having given the little girl sundry directions as to the assumption of preternatural virtue, the woman commenced to read.

Masters resumed his place at the other end of the seat. Had book in hand too: manuscript book. He had come out with intent to write; told himself that fulfilment was necessary. But he had Gracie to reckon with.

The sharp eyes of that four-year-old little maid were furtively fixed on the magic pen. She was trying hard to fulfil the injunction: Be good—from the adult standpoint. But gradually the admonition was fading from her mind— she was very human.

After a while—a courage-summoning period—the little hands were laced behind her, and boldly facing the owner of the attraction, the little one addressed him, in a kind of I Dare You voice:

"I could write with a pen like that!"

For a second time the child's voice brought the man's attention away from his work.

"Could you?"

He smiled as he spoke. Looked up from his book as he did so. Then, infusing a note of doubt in his voice, enquired:

"Are you sure?"

"Y—yes. Quite!"

Then, as an afterthought, possibly by way of redemption of the hesitation, the child continued:

"I could if I had one!"

Finding her first venture had not roused the lion, but fearing him a little still, she went on defiantly:

"I saw a man fill one once!"

Such a statement as that surely could not fail to crush a mere user of the pen! Seeing that astonishment was expected of him, Masters assumed an appropriate look of surprise. His wearing of it pleased her mightily.

"Perhaps," he said, "you would like to make quite sure you could write with one, eh? Would you like to try with this?"

The blue eyes brightened; she was at his side in a moment. Shyness is readily overcome when our summers have not numbered five. Trustfulness at that age has rarely been shocked.

Therein, perhaps, lay the secret of the attraction children had for Masters: the sweetness of their suspicionless existence. Viewed from the standpoint of the after life, when—if we act up to the axioms of the world we live in— we trust no man, it is apt to brush across us as refreshingly as a gust of country air.

Turning the leaves of his book till he came to a blank page, Masters twisted and rested the cover on his knee. So the open leaf was level with the intending—eyes-sparkling-with-excitement—writer. Then he gave the child his pen.

She drew a capital G—a bright little point of tongue protruding the while. The head, too, seemed to follow the movements of the hand. Her intent was plain: to write her own name.

That was compassed. It took a little time—entailed a huge expenditure of concentrated energy—but she got through with it at last. There figured on the paper the words:

Gracie Seton-Carr.

The child's glance came off the page; she moved away a pace. Looked up into his eyes, her own flashing like diamonds. Such little things please—in that time of happiness when we are little ourselves. After drawing a long breath she ejaculated triumphantly:

"There!"

Once more Masters gladdened the little one, by acting as he was expected to act. No man on that coast could have worn a larger-sized look of astonishment. He cried:

"Won—der—ful!"

A clapping of hands in her glee, and the child danced merrily along to the other end of the seat.

"I've written my name with one of those funny squirter pens, Miss Mivvins! What do you think of that?"

"I think you have a funny way of keeping your word, Gracie. You professed anxiety to finish your castle on the sands, yet you are spending your time on the wall!"

"Oh-h-h!"—prolonged and drawn out—"I had forgotten all about it!"

Attention diverted from the pen, the child ran down the steps on to the beach. A few minutes after, Masters, looking up, saw her busily at work with a spade and pail. The implements had evidently been left there in the morning.

That rather proved the excellence of the estimate the author had made of Wivernsea out of the season. Castle builders could leave their tools uncared for and find them when they returned. Not because of a superabundance of honesty around; rather because of the lack of thieves.

The castle creator continued her work; the pail-shaped battlements increased in number. She handled bucket and spade with the same earnestness, eagerness and engrossment with which she had fingered the pen.

Those were methods which appealed to the story-creator. But just now he was not working with his own accustomed engrossment, eagerness and earnestness. A disturbing element had crept in.

From time to time he glanced towards the other end of the seat. There the disturbing element lay: or rather sat. It seemed that there was something magnetic about that presence there. He experienced a difficulty in keeping his eyes away. Noting the neatness of the dress worn by the woman, he could not fail to note too its sombre hue: mourning evidently. His lively imagination was busily at work in a moment.

For him to weave a complete story with such material, was an easy task. A pretty girl occupied the stellar part in it. He portrayed her as a motherless one forced to face a hard, cold world. Depicted her seeking a living in it as a governess.

That imagination of his had a habit of running away with him. Perhaps that was a reason why his fiction had so good a run. His books were mostly all of the many-editioned kind. So, neglecting his own story for fiction of another kind, the time came of the going down of the sun. The tint of the vasty-deep changed: the sea grew greyer. His heroine-presumptive closed her book and rose; cried:

"Gracie!"

Seeing that the child's attention had been attracted, she turned, and bowing slightly, smilingly wished Masters:

"Good-day!"

From the sands, the little girl waved a vigorous cumbered-with-bucket-and-spade good-bye to him. She evidently preferred jumping the breakwaters on the way home to the more easy path of the sea wall. The two passed altogether from the author's sight. Not altogether from his mind.

Good-day! Yes, he felt it had been—distinctly good. Till he looked at clean pages, where writing should have been. Even then, despite the unfinished chapter, he made no alteration in his verdict.

It had been a good day.

CHAPTER III

SHE DISCOVERS THE AUTHOR

For nearly a week—before and after noon—they met. It was a sheltered spot Miss Mivvins walked out to each day. She had selected it on account of its freedom from cold winds: there was a seat on which to sit and read. At the same time a watchful eye could be kept on her playing-on-the-sands charge.

Masters had always used it. Neither now gave it up because of the other. Each would have scornfully repudiated a suggestion that the regular seeking of it arose from any other reason. For instance, that it could be ascribed to the other's presence.

But would the repudiation have been honestly grounded? Cupid alone knows. The love-god is a deity enshrined in mystery. He never reveals the secrets of the wonders he performs. Were it possible to see the hand which lets loose the arrow, probably there would be many a stepping aside to avoid it. The sudden striking of the dart makes it so deadly—wounds to the heart.

Gracie and the author became fast friends. She was a winsome little soul, and children have their own methods of creating friendships. Masters met her advances more than half-way: was as fond of children as he was of flowers.

His friends—the nice friends who feel privileged to say nasty things—by reason of that fondness, professed to see in it a chance of his redemption. They admitted a possibility of his becoming humanized some day: said there was at least hope for him.

Beyond a Good Morning, and occasionally a remark on one of the tenses of the weather—past, present or future—the meetings were bare of conversation, so far as the adults were concerned.

Masters would have been more than glad to talk. Perhaps natural nervousness prevented his setting the conversational ball rolling. For he admired his companion of the seat with a fervent admiration—unable to label the feeling, as yet, by any other name.

Her presence did not disturb him now in his seclusion. She seemed to be in keeping with his thoughts. His thoughts of her harmonized with the surroundings—she belonged to them.

A vague sort of wonder took possession of him; how it was that he had never missed her—never known what was lacking. The more he saw of her, the more deep his admiration grew.

Admiration is the kind of thing which develops rapidly, once it germinates. In this instance the seed had thrown deep roots. Masters' heart seemed likely to prove fruitful soil.

With Gracie he stood well. That, he felt, was a making of headway; for the governess unquestionably loved her charge. On the principle of love me, love my dog, he was acting wisely—apart from the pleasure it gave him—in this cultivation of the little one's affection.

When the child discovered his ability to manufacture stories she instantly— the exacting nature of her sex in its dealings with man manifested itself even at that early age—demanded to be told one.

That was the introduction of the wedge's thin end: brought about a little change in the current of the elders' conversation. The lady in black came out of the ice-bound silence—fringed by a frigid Good Morning and Good Afternoon; saying:

"You must not let Gracie worry you."

The lashes went up as she spoke and he got a good view of those lovely eyes of hers. They held him spellbound. The evident admiration in his glance caused the lashes to fall, and he, released from the momentary thraldom, exclaimed:

"Worry! How could she?"

"She is a perfect little glutton for stories. Once you indulge her, she will do her best to make your life unbearable with her clamour for more. With food of that sort within reach she is a regular Oliver Twist."

A gratified little laugh—he thought he saw the door to Friendship opening a little wider—accompanied his answer:

"Oh, story-telling is in my particular line! I am full of fiction to the brim!"

She reciprocated his laugh, and as she picked up, to resume, her book, said:

"Well, I have warned you! The consequences be on your own head."

"I am moved to disregard your warning! Gracie is so excellent a listener. That is so flattering, you know." Then turning to the child, he continued: "Now, run on to the sands and finish your castle, little woman, before the tide reaches it. When it can no longer withstand Old Ocean's assaults and is washed away, come back. Then I will tell you what became of Jack after the fairy had rescued him from the three-headed giant."

The child was sitting on his knee with her arms round his neck. Between the kisses she was giving him, said:

"You dear old thing! You are the very nicest, delightfullest, beautifullest story-teller I ever met."

"I am dethroned then?" The observation from Miss Mivvins. "I used to be told that."

"Y-y-yes. But you never told me tales like Prince Charlie's."

Prince Charlie was a character in one of the stories Masters had told the child. A prince who had rescued innumerable princesses from giants, ogres and demons. Instantly it had pleased the listener to christen the narrator after the hero.

All her people, she informed him gravely, she christened out of stories. It was much nicer than calling them by their real names. They were so much prettier and lots easier to remember—didn't he think so?

Yes, he had made answer. He quite thought that Prince Charlie was an improvement on his own name. But Gracie betrayed no anxiety to know what that was. To her henceforth he was Prince Charlie. That was quite sufficient—she was a godmother of the most self-satisfied type.

Turning to Miss Mivvins the child continued, with a trace of reproach in her voice—she felt she had been defrauded:

"Besides, your giants never had three heads!"

A trinity of that description—unity is strength—appeared an unanswerable argument; seemed to her to clinch the matter. She climbed down from Masters' knee, and jumped her way down the steps to the sands, with bucket and spade rattling in her little hand.

As she disappeared, Masters took his courage in both hands; a trifle nervously continued the conversation:

"I shall have to prescribe a course of Grimm's *Fairy Tales*, if you wish to resume your position as story-teller-in-chief."

His speech was at random. The ice was broken; they had spoken; he did not want the coldness of silence to freeze it all over again. Having got in the thin edge of the wedge he proposed to drive it right home—if possible. Hence his speech.

Miss Mivvins laughed. The child liked him—so did she. Fearful of driving her away, he had not attempted to force conversation. She had curled up a trifle because of his reserve—hence they had spoken but little. Unknown to themselves their communication had been more subtle than that of words, perhaps had paved the way for them. They came easily enough now.

"You also," he said, "seem to have a taste for fiction of a pronounced type. I see you are reading one of my books."

"Your books?" Her query was uttered in a tone of surprise. "Oh, no! This came down from Mudie's with other volumes yesterday."

"Oh, I don't doubt that."

He laughed openly at her concern—a hearty, resounding laugh, a trifle loud, but with a pleasant honest ring in it; continued:

"I don't doubt that the library people acquired it honestly. My claim was not made in a possessory sense. I meant that my name figures on the title page."

She looked at him blankly for a moment, so great was her surprise. Then, the truth dawning on her, she said:

"You! You—are the author?"

CHAPTER IV

THE DANGER SIGNAL

That she should meet a real live author, the writer of the book she was reading, was a coincidence strange enough to take Miss Mivvins' breath away. Masters saw her wonderment, smiled at it.

"Is the fact," he asked, "so difficult a thing to reconcile with my appearance?"

"Oh, no, no! How awfully rude you must think me! I meant—I mean—that I expected the author of this book to be——"

Then she paused. Did not quite know what she expected or how to express herself; added lamely:

"To be much older."

"Really! I am sorry I don't come up to your age standard. Age has its privileges, but wisdom is not always its perquisite. Why should an author be necessarily old? Surely youth is pardonable?"

She—a woman famous in her own particular circle for the coolness of her tongue—could have kicked herself. Was saying, in her unwonted nervousness, all the things she would rather have left unsaid. Angry with herself, she blurted out:

"There is not, of course, any earthly reason why. It was purely my utter stupidity."

He smiled at the flush on her cheek; a smile conjured up by his admiration of it; said merrily:

"Here have I been peacocking around, with a sort of metaphorical feather in my cap. Pampering my vanity, applying the flattering unction to my soul—rubbing it in several times per diem—that no author of my age has turned out so many volumes. Lo! with one breath you blow that feather clean away."

She could not resist laughing at his mock despair. Became at her ease once more; said:

"Indeed not! I don't know what prompted me to say what I did. As to this book——"

"No! Don't! Please don't give me your opinion of it!"

His interruption was a continuance of his burlesque melodramatic style. She did not quite know how to take him; said:

"You mean you would not value my opinion?"

That was disconcerting. Sobered him in a minute. He knew quite well the kind of value he would be likely to put on any opinion of hers—concerning himself.

"Oh, no!" His answer was spoken earnestly. "I do not mea——"

But she interrupted him. In her nervousness felt that whilst her tongue was in action it would help to keep the helm the right way; said:

"Why should you? A stranger's opinion would necessarily be valueless. You know nothing of me."

The deafness of those who will not hear is proverbial. The underlying earnestness in the tone of his reply should have warned her.

"Aren't you going just a trifle too far?" he asked. "We are not quite strangers. True, I know nothing of you—except that you are Miss Mivvins."

An irresistible smile accompanied his words. His smile—and his laugh too—were capable of creating many friends. But he did not allow them to. His views on the subject of friendship were cynical in the extreme.

His smile was infectious. Once more those alluring dimples which he had noticed at their first meeting deepened in her face.

"It is distinctly more my misfortune than my fault," he continued, "that I know so little of you. May I say—with an absence of fear of your thinking me impertinent—that I should like, much like, to know more of you?"

The flush, that becoming flush, on her cheek again. The eyes were fringed over by those long lashes of hers as she cast them groundwards. Just a blend of trouble in her look as she queried:

"Really?"

He liked the pink showing on the white. Colours inspire some men. Perhaps the combination in her face inspired him. Anyway, there was more vigour and determination in his voice as he answered:

"Yes."

She, dallying, as a woman will, quite well knew that there was a spark. That it would burst into flame, chose she to fan it; gained time by asking:

"Why?"

He vaulted on to his hobby horse. The question was a stirrup helping him to the saddle.

"Because I—may I say it?—hail you in a measure as a kindred soul."

She lifted her eyes; he could not fail to read the astonishment filling them; continued:

"You are here in October, and you don't look bored; don't look as if life held no further charm for you. You do not follow the fashionable decrying of the place simply because it is out of fashion—*because* it is October."

She smiled. Encouraged by it, he continued, in the same strain:

"You are always alone, yet you create the impression that you are happy. You don't seem to sigh for bands of music, to hanker after a crowded promenade. You find existence possible without a shoal of people to help you pass your time."

Her smile broadened into a laugh. This time at herself—at his description of her; she asked:

"And those—shall I call them unusual?—characteristics in a woman interest you?"

"Amazingly!"

"Why?"

She put the question with a little nervousness, bred of that eagerness of his.

"Because—well, let me say by sheer force of contrast. In those respects, Heaven be thanked, you are not as other women."

The amused look had not left her face. It lingered in the upward curve of the corners of her eyes.

"So you prefer eccentric women, then?"

She could not resist just a trace of mischief in the tone of her query. He answered:

"Heaven forefend! I see nothing eccentric in the attributes I have allotted to you. They are refreshingly good to a thirsty soul."

The amusement and mischief tones left her voice. She asked demurely:

"Are you thirsty?"

"Parched! I confess I am. I have just escaped from the dead level of dry conventionality. That arid desert: the Sahara of Society. Its womenkind are my abomination."

She looked a little annoyed. As if not appreciating his description.

"I have heard it rumoured, Mr. Masters, that you fly from London to escape Society's attentions."

"And for once the many-tongued is not a lying jade. I suppose all of us, every man and woman, are more or less eccentric."

"Put it that we, most of us, have bees in our bonnets."

"Precisely. The buzzing of my particular insect is the artificial life of modern Society. I just loathe it; never go out for that reason. Fly from London? Yes; I own up; I do. As fast as an express can wing me. Fly to escape the inanities with which the cup of social life is overflowing."

"Balls, parties——"

"And things of that sort are my pet horrors."

She smiled at the expression of his disgust; his manner of expressing it; said:

"I seem to be shaking a red rag at a bull!"

"If," he continued, "Society is the product of civilization I am an untutored savage. Not an ungrateful one, mark you, but one thankful for his savagery. Afternoon teas, flower shows, and the hundred and one idiotic things which go to make up the ordinary every-day life in London ought to be abolished by a drastic Act of Parliament."

Her smile merged into laughter. She had gauged his capacity for exaggeration by this time. The beginning of her understanding of him was setting in. Her laugh over, she said:

"I think you are very drastic."

"I hope not!"

"Why?"

"Because if you think so, I have been mistaken. I have formed a wrong estimate of your character if you care for those things."

"And supposing I did? Would it be, think you—unwomanly?"

"As the world wags? No. On the contrary. The absolute quintessence of womanliness in nine hundred and ninety-nine women out of a possible thousand."

"But——"

"Ah! that is it!"

"But if I did care for all and singular the things you object to so much?"

"I should be sorry—really sorry—that I had spoken as I have done."

"Why?"

"Because it would, must, savour of impertinence. We, each of us, have a right to our own opinions. I should just hate to think that I have been forcing mine on any one; it would be a painful thing. Opinions, like boots, should fit the wearer—neither too narrow nor too wide, and possibly an allowance for stretching a point. To force an opinion would be a modernized version of the iron boot the torturers used to handle in the Inquisition days."

"But you expressed yourself"—she smiled at the recollection of it—"very strongly just now."

"Because I thought we were more or less on the same plane; were thinking in common. I hoped so."

"Tell me, will you, why you thought me different from other women: thought as you did of me?"

"Oh, come! Isn't that now—don't you think that rather hard on me?"

"Why?"

"To put such a question as that. Calling on me to tell you why I think."

"Why not?"

"Think! If I could bring myself to lie you would not like it. Yet, supposing I said something to offend you?"

"Why should you?"

"Because of my ignorance. I would not for worlds—knowingly. You would know that I should not mean to."

"Very well, then. Why should I take offence where none is intended?"

He hesitated a moment. Plainly saw the danger-signal flying; then he spoke:

"You are a woman."

She tossed her head at that. There was no mistaking the tone in which she said:

"Thank you!"

"There!... Proof positive! I won't speak; I won't risk it. I am most anxious not to offend you, and you shan't force my hand."

She tapped impatiently with the toe of her shoe.

CHAPTER V

PLAYING WITH FIRE

Miss Mivvins was annoyed; the impatient tapping was evidence of it. Not that a little exhibition of temper in any way detracted from her personal appearance. On the contrary, the air of petulance heightened her charms.

"You are just like a man!"

Her speech was accompanied by another toss of her shapely head.

"Isn't that twisting things round? You mean that he never gives a reason for what he says or does?"

"Yes."

Resumption of tattoo with her foot on the ground. It made him exclaim:

"I knew I was right! What if I tell you that I am a mind reader?"

"I would not be a bit surprised!"

He was: greatly. Could not understand what she meant; queried:

"You wouldn't?"

"No."

"I am—to hear you say it. Why?"

"Because in this book of yours I am reading"—she held it up—"I see you believe in palmistry."

"Come, come!" He was genuine in his expostulation. "I make one of my characters believe in it."

"Then you do not?"

She had him in a corner; was merciless. He tried to wriggle out; said:

"I did not say so."

It was an infecund effort on his part. She pinned him in still further; was that kind of woman.

"What does that mean? That you do and you do not?"

There was nothing for him but to fence; he answered:

"Yes and No."

It did not in any way extricate him from his difficulty. She continued:

"You are a complete enigma."

"There is no prize offered for the solution."

He endeavoured to speak lightly, to bring the conversation back to the humorous line it had left; continued:

"I have known people take quite an interest in enigmas. Do you?"

She changed the subject. Kept away from where there was a treading on dangerous ground; felt the ice getting thin; said:

"I gather that this palmist character of yours professes to read the past, but does not venture on prophecy?"

"I venture on prophecy now!"

He spoke suddenly, rising as he did so. Picking up his books, and—for the first time—quietly possessing himself of her bag, continued:

"That rapidly travelling cloud, at present looking very little larger than a man's hand, coming from the south, is full of rain. It will burst before we are back in the town, unless we hurry. Gracie! Gracie!"

The little girl came running in response to his call. All three, for the first time, walked homewards together. A student of human nature might have seen in it a beginning of things.

"I am living in Marine Terrace."

He was describing the situation of his lodgings. Waited for her to respond, and then asked:

"Have you far to go?"

"Oh, not so far as you have; little more than half-way. Ivy Cottage; on the front. Do you know——"

"That pretty little bungalow with the creeper over the porch? Before we reach the big houses?"

"Yes."

He cast an eye over his shoulder at the still distant cloud, gauging the time of its breaking; said:

"When the rain comes it will last, I fear. That will mean confinement to the house."

"I fancy so, too. The local weatherwise are predicting it also. You are not the only prophet. 'Corns are shooting and roomatiz is bad.'"

He laughed at her excellent imitation of the dialect ruling the language of the people; then said:

"May I be personal? How are you off for reading matter?"

"Oh, Mudie's have sent me down an absolutely abominable selection. With"—a twinkle escaped from the corner of her eye—"with the exception of that one of yours."

"I won't gratify you with even a smile of approval at so callous a joke," he said coolly. "To trample on my feelings so is positively inhuman. Still, that 'exception' emboldens me."

"In what way?"

"That finding you interested in one of my books, I want you to let me—I want you to favour me by accepting from me a set?"

"A set?"

"I have been guilty of five others." Mock despair was in his tone. "Accept my contrite apologies."

"Five others!"

"I have to plead guilty to that number. Heinous, isn't it?"

"Oh, I did not mean that."

"And so young too!"

"Really, Mr. Masters!" The flush was being worn again. "You are, really, too bad; raking up old grievances!"

"I would like you to try and think there is a substratum of good."

She ignored his speech, rather the significance in the tone of its delivery; said:

"I did not know—I confess openly, you see. This makes but the third of yours I have read."

"Then there is a possibility of interest being left in the three you have not read. Let the weather be my excuse for forcing them on you."

"As if an excuse were needed! Pray do not speak of your kindness so!"

"Then—I have some work I must finish this afternoon for the post—may I bring them to you this evening?"

She hesitated a moment. Induced to do so by a thought of the unwisdom of playing with fire. His hyper-sensitive nature made him shrink from that hesitation, to nervously say:

"I beg your pardon. I mean I will make a parcel of them and send them up to you."

The note of pain in his voice was so plain that any question of her wisdom—or want of it—vanished. She was moved to put her hand on his arm; to say:

"Don't deprive me of half the pleasure of the gift. Please bring them yourself."

It was a pretty little speech. Prettily spoken. No answering word came to his lips, but the look of gladness in his eyes was eloquent. Eloquent enough to make her mentally pause again and ask herself: was she acting altogether wisely?

Miss Mivvins was sailing under false colours. Was not in a position to haul them down, or fly her own. But she found him entertaining and—and—and very pleasant to talk to. She left it at that.

She could not afterwards remember much of what they talked about on their walk along the wall homewards. But she was conscious of spending a very pleasant afternoon; that it had passed away all too quickly. The most entertaining conversations are usually those which flow so smoothly that we forget to note the landmarks and stepping-stones on the way.

She was in a quandary: dared not reveal to him her true self. She had learnt enough of him to know that if she ran up her own flag, one glance at the masthead would mean his sheering right away.

She was not at all anxious that that should happen; did not want to lose him. She had grown to—to—to more than like him. Why, she asked herself petulantly, why could he not be as other men?

The rain held off till they reached her gate. There they said good-bye, shaking hands for the first time. The touch thrilled them both. As an outcome he saw possibilities; felt what their meeting might possibly lead to. It was a pleasant feeling. Things were coloured by it—colour of the rose.

Her good-bye was spoken lightly. Instinctively she tried to counteract that thrill. Yet there was a lingering tone in her voice as she said, finally:

"Till eight o'clock."

Then came Gracie's turn. He stooped down, lifted and kissed her. She said—

"Good-bye, Prince Charlie. I shan't see you in the evening because I go to bed at half-past seven."

"My word! Half-past seven! How late for a little girl to sit up!"

She exclaimed indignantly at so gross an insult:

"I'm not a little girl! I'm nearly five!"

Her indignation was a fleeting one. He held her away; threw her up in the air till she screamed with the delight of the pleasant fear. Then caught and kissed her and set the mite on her feet again.

So he dealt with the child. Then, raising his hat, gave a final kindly smile in the direction of the governess; nodded and said a final good-bye.

Such was their parting. Each was full of thoughts of the other. He walked home wonderingly, thinking, why—for what reason—she had said eight o'clock. It sounded so—then he laughed at his stupid thought.

So life touches life a moment, thrills and bids it stay—as two drops of water in a peaceful stream may touch for an instant and in the next be parted by the waving reeds.

What of after meetings? Would they be guided to one another by that strange fate that we call Destiny?

CHAPTER VI

A STRANGE REQUEST

As a weather prophet Masters proved more reliable than those who fill a like mission on the daily papers.

It rained heavily all the afternoon. His landlady when she brought in his tea remarked that it was pouring cats and dogs—the latter, presumably, of the Skye terrier breed.

A temporary clearance of the weather came about in the evening. Masters was glad; he went to Ivy Cottage. The bungalow-like building was curiously situate in its own square piece of grass land, fronting the sea. The back of the house looked on to the road leading to the railway station a little distance away. Admission to the cottage was gained by doors at back and front of it.

The house agent entrusted with the letting of the place had described it as possessed of advantages not to be passed over lightly. There was one—an unsurpassed convenience in the matter of not missing a train—that certainly was undeniable and evident.

So close was the back of the house to the railway that from the windows an approaching train could be seen in time enough to allow of easy walking to catch it. Masters walked up the gravel path to the front door. Touched the push of the bell.... A trim maid-servant responded. He enquired:

"Miss Mivvins—is she within?"

The girl started. Hesitated as she looked at him closely—doubtfully—for a moment. Then opened a side door in the hall, requesting him to enter and be seated.

It was a charmingly arranged room to which he was thus introduced. Evidenced woman in every insignificant little detail; her gentle touch was visible in all things. He thought of the touch of one woman in particular.

Miss Mivvins' spirit seemed to have impressed itself in every fold of the curtains; in all the quiet harmony of colouring; in the inexpensive simplicity of the whole—as distinct from cheapness.

Expensive simplicity often stamps the quality of a room; it was not to be seen here. There was nothing cheap about the furnishing; nothing meretricious; nothing to catch the eye. Nothing of the enamel paint and varnish description; all in that apartment was plainly and simply what it represented itself to be; its keynote: truth.

Masters was astonished. Because he had no idea that such signs of refinement existed in Wivernsea. But then he knew its lodging houses only—where the great god is Aspinall and an uneasy chair the only attempt at comfort.

He sat some moments waiting. Whilst doing so, he thought again of the curious way in which the maid had looked at him. Perhaps Miss Mivvins was in a less comfortable place than he had thought. He had judged by the freedom she enjoyed, that no possible harm could result from his visit to her. Was he wrong?

Perhaps that accounted for her hesitation, when he had suggested calling with the books. What a fool he had been, not to think of that! Perhaps she would get into trouble by reason of his visit to her employer's house.

The more he thought of this the more uncomfortable he became. As a result of his deliberations, determined that he would make his stay a short and formal one. There could surely be no harm accrue to her from that.

The rustle of a woman's dress warned him of her approach. Presently she entered. The moment his eyes rested on her he was amazed: she was dressed so perfectly. No scrap of colour; no scintillation of a jewel.

He had a mere man's eye for woman's dress—sensible of the tout ensemble, not of detail—but he did not despise it. It seemed fitting to him that graceful women should be gracefully attired.

All harmony was grateful to his soul; it did not seem unnatural for Miss Mivvins to be gowned in accordance with her beauty. Still he experienced astonishment, grave astonishment, when she entered.

For the life of him he could not have defined the impression which took hold of him. But he knew that her gown was of some soft, rich, silken, costly texture. Resultant upon that was the belief that her place must be an easier one than he had begun to think it.

The extension of her hand to him. Once more with it in his own, he felt thrilled. That feeling and his previous resolve to hurry away did not blend well. The thrill remained; the resolve faded.

He produced the books he had promised to bring with him. On the fly-leaf of each he had written her name; beneath it had appended his signature. So many people bothered him for autograph copies of his books, that it was a pardonable vanity if he had begun to think there was something around his signature which enhanced the value of his works. So he had penned the words, *With kindest regards, from the Author*, between her name and his own.

At sight of what he had written she laughed. At first, gently; a gentleness which passed into real hearty mirth. Then, catching sight of his face, the laugh died away ashamedly! Had she whipped him he could not have looked more hurt. His hyper-sensitive nature was suffering.

That laughter acted on Masters as if the ceiling had opened and a shower of cold water had fallen—his face showed it. To be the subject of mirth was a novelty to him. He was glad that that was so. Felt that it was not a pleasant sensation to experience. That a very little of it went an extremely long way.

She flushed with annoyance at her own rudeness; with shame for having wounded the feelings of her visitor. He had not the faintest idea why she laughed, of course; want of knowledge so often leads to misunderstanding. She said hurriedly:

"I hope you do not—oh, how can I explain what I was laughing at? Mr. Masters, don't, pray don't—I beg of you—think I was rude—intended to be rude—or that I was laughing at anything even remotely connected with these books, which, believe me, I shall always value, always prize."

That earnest humble little speech of hers did not sponge away the look from his face. In her eagerness to acquit herself she placed her hand on his arm—it was for the second time that day. It was a habit of hers when moved. Was quite an innocent gesture; but there was—in his estimation, anyway—a distinct piquancy about its naturalness.

"Oh—Mr. Masters!"

She got as far as that. Then stood at a loss for words. She had spoken in such dead earnest tones that it would have been absurd to think her lying. Finding her tongue again, she continued:

"Pray, pray believe me! I was stupid, I know, but don't be so hard as to think me capable of insulting you. Don't! Please, don't!"

His forgiveness was hers that moment. The wonder remained what she could have laughed at—but all else was forgotten. She had looked into his eyes—a pretty woman's trick, mostly always successful. When performed with such eyes as Miss Mivvins' failure was absolutely impossible.

"I don't think you rude. Don't think you insulting. I could not think any ill thing of you if I tried."

She had badly wanted to hear just some such thing. But there was that in the tone in which he spoke it that made her flush again. She drew in her breath; drew back a little.

"I am so glad!"

Miss Mivvins spoke impetuously—nervously. She to be nervous! And that, too, in speaking to such a boyish, ingenuous individual as was Masters! It was quite too absurd! She continued:

"I—I should not like you to think badly of me."

She was obviously ill at ease—the obviousness was the worst part of it. She knew that herself; knew quite well. It was because he believed in her! Because he trusted her so implicitly; had an almost childlike faith in her.

With all the other men she had known, on whom she had exerted the power of her fascination, her woman's ways and wiles had seemed fair and fitting. They were but part of the game, and understood by both sides of it. The men had been men of the world—her world—armed and armoured against her coquetry and charm.

Flirtation in those instances had been carried to the point of a fine art—it was part of the life she lived. But it had been flirtation, pure and simple. Though it was amusing enough while it lasted, it had been fencing with blunt points.

No one had any wounds—not a scratch. Experience had taught them all to play the game skilfully. No one had been deceived into taking things seriously. No soul was a scrap the worse.

But Masters was of another world than hers. Superficiality seemed unknown to him; he put his heart into what he said and did. Playing with life was evidently a thing unknown to him; he was in earnest; always would be; that was his temperament. Honest himself, he believed her to be likewise.

What a character! Of course it appealed to her—she would not have been a woman if it had not. He would face her woman's weapons—even her most innocent little deceptions—unsuspecting; unarmed. To shower on him the full force of her artillery would be grossly unfair.

She was constrained to throw off the conventional. To don the mantle of guilelessness—such as he wore himself. He made it impossible for her to act otherwise. But the experience was quite a new one to her; it was the novelty that made her nervous. To be trusted—implicitly—was delightfully disconcerting.

Her manner filled Masters with wonder. The key to the mysterious nervousness was not in his possession. Again there flitted across his mind the idea that it arose from his visit to her employer's house.

His resolution to stay but a little time occurred to him. It would be best to go. Yet he abhorred the idea of so speedy a parting; if only he could——
He paused. Thought a moment. Risked it; said tentatively:

"The rain has ceased. It is damp below but bright above."

A pause. His reference to the weather seemed out of place. She did not know the difficulty he was experiencing in screwing his courage to the sticking place. He continued:

"I am walking to the end of the parade and back."

Having voiced as much, his conversational powers failed him. He somehow hoped that she would suggest joining him in his walk. That his ignorance of women was of vast magnitude was evidenced by the nature of that hope.

He was very transparent—so much so that there was no difficulty in guessing his thoughts. She smiled. Ingenuousness was scarcely the word for him! He should have known the impossibility of her offering to accompany him, however much she might desire to do so. As she did not speak he went even further, saying, with nervous awkwardness:

"It is a warm evening—will you walk with me?"

The smile left her face and her eyes opened wide. She was startled at the suddenness of his request. Still more at the nature of it. Then remembered the nature of the man. Felt too that there was owing to him something for that unkind laugh of hers. Then there was the trend of her own feelings. After a moment she tossed discretion to the winds; said:

"I shall be glad to—if you wish it!"

The words spoken, she was amazed at their utterance. Her ready acquiescence pleased him. It voiced that honesty he thought so precious in her, which was so sadly lacking in other women. He suspected that another member of her sex would have raised scruples, merely that he might flatter himself that he had overcome them.

The absence of such coquetry in Miss Mivvins was refreshing—refreshing as the rays of the sun after electric light. So he likened her womanhood to other women's. He little knew what a whited sepulchre she felt herself to be. His admiration of what she did not possess positively hurt her.

Leaving the room for outdoor covering, she presently returned with a long warm cloak and her hat. Had got them from the hall; came back with them over her arm. Having agreed to accompany him, she lost no time.

He assisted her to put on the cloak: an expensive, fur-lined wrap. He could not but notice that as, with trembling fingers—a nervousness born of his touch of her—he helped to button the garment down the front.

Microbes multiply in darkness; sunlight kills them. Her natural manner, open as day, crushed the germ of suspicion. They left the house and walked along the parade: in the direction of the seat at the end of it.

CHAPTER VII

READING THE HAND

The moon was now shining, now obscured. A capricious, gusty wind played fantastic tricks with dark clouds across its face. But by the time the eastern end of the sea wall was reached the Goddess of Night had risen clear; was shining brightly. She silvered and lighted up the rippling waters: jewelling it as only the moon can.

"Shall we rest for a few minutes?"

The suggestion was Masters'. Not that he was tired. But he had that on his mind to unload, which he felt would be easier of utterance sitting down.

They sat. After an awkward interval—she was afraid to help him—he spoke again. Not without difficulty. Love-making in his novels he had found the easiest part of his writing. He was finding reality a steed of a totally different colour.

In an imaginative man it is possible for imagination to be more real than reality; just as a painting may give a truer impression than a photograph. To Masters, just now, reality seemed frigid and limited. He felt himself bound: tied down to—and by—hard-and-fast lines.

Then again there was the horrible uncertainty: he was not sure. It was necessary to feel his way. He had heard her laugh once. He did not need a second edition of that—with himself filling the rôle of laughee. He had no desire to figure as a larger-sized ass than was possible. Putting stripes on a donkey does not make a zebra of it. He said slowly:

"I have been here, to Wivernsea, regularly for years past. Have sat on this seat scores and scores of times. Now—I shall never forget Wivernsea or this seat."

That was his heavily-shod method of feeling his way; of nearly putting his foot into it. She afforded him no fragment of assistance; being a woman, of course help was not to be expected of her. Woman is an enigma; sympathetic to the point of soft-as-silk, heart bleeding; yet there are times when she finds pleasure in a man's agony. Masters' speech simply elicited the query:

"Why?"

He gathered boldness from the sheer impudence of her question. Felt that it was impossible that she could have misunderstood; said:

"I shall always link the place—and the seat—with thoughts of you."

Her impudence had limits. She could not affect to misunderstand that. Besides, the accelerated beating of her heart warned her. She must change the subject.

"The last time we were sitting here, Mr. Masters, you hurriedly broke into the subject of palmistry, with wise prophecies of bad weather."

"Realized prophecies! Give me that credit!"

"Certainly; you deserve it! But tell me now—quite seriously—do you believe in palmistry?"

The dexterous turning of the subject annoyed him. He was, however, compelled to reply to her question; said:

"Seriously? Well, to an extent—yes."

"Really?"

"Oh, don't think I go too far! Don't for a moment suppose that I am pretending that the geography of the future, mountains, plains—the ups and downs of life—can be studied from the map of the hand."

"And yet I have heard——"

"Charlatans profess to do so? Oh, yes; scores of them. I can understand a nimble-witted, half-a-guinea—or a guinea if she can get it—Regent Street sibyl professing so. That is fraud; absolute downright fraud. But I believe that much of a man's or woman's temperament, disposition, call it what you will, can be plainly read from the lines of the hand."

"Read mine."

She spoke impulsively. Persuasively too, the while she pulled off her glove. Palmistry, if it does not truly predict fate, is ofttimes responsible for much of its direction.

To hold her warm little hand in his—she had kept it close within the recesses of her muff—was much too good an opportunity to let slip. He bent over; spent quite a time on the study of the lines on her palm. He had only the light of the moon to work by; perhaps that accounted for the time expenditure; or perhaps he—well, anyway, he was holding her hand all the while.

During the task—it was a silent one—he was tempted, sore, to put his lips in the warm centre of what he held. Possibly she divined that; gathered it perhaps from the trembling of his fingers as they grasped her own. Stiffening a little, she queried:

"Well?"

Her voice was as the application of a brake; pulled him up. Tightening his hold on himself he loosened his tongue.

"Temperament first," he answered. "Passionate—wilful—affectionate—hasty——"

The reading was wound up at that point. The cataloguer paused, as it were, in the middle of his list. In astonishment she asked:

"Why do you stop? Is that all you can read?"

"No—no. But my belief—my faith—is shaken!"

Just a faint tremor in the voice—it was not unnoticed by him—as she asked:

"Faith? In what?"

He fenced. Did not like to shape words around what he thought he read. The truth is not always pleasant. So it was that he answered:

"Palmistry as a science."

The woman's voice was steadied again. There was a ring of merriment in it, ridiculing his seriousness, as she said—

"Why this shaken faith? Because of what you read in my hand?"

"M'yes."

"Tell me——"

"No. What I have read—the indications—I know to be wrong. This is a rude shock to my credence! I shall never again believe in palmistry's infallibility!"

"Tell me?"

She spoke impatiently; her curiosity was well aroused. Scrutinizing her hand with interest; wholly disbelieving him, she said imperatively:

"What do you read?"

"There seemed to be indicated characteristics there, the exact opposite of those you possess."

"Tell me?"

"No."

She drew her hand away a trifle angrily: obstinacy opposed to curiosity is as flint to steel. Fingers, trembling a little, began putting on her glove. The look in her eyes could not be truthfully described as softness; all the same it was very becoming.

He was not insensible of her feeling, for the birth of which he was responsible. Just restrained her: put his hand out on to hers. A simple act, but one he performed more gravely than the occasion warranted; said:

"Don't be angry."

Then hesitated; conscious, now he had spoken, that the admonition—by presupposing cause for it—was not likely to improve matters. Felt that he had put a large-sized foot into it.

"Angry!"

The glitter in her eyes, as she repeated his word, warned him that his intuition was correct; made him say:

"Well—annoyed."

"You are so—so provoking!"

"I am sorry——"

"No, you are not! You are not sorry a little bit!"

"Believe me——"

"If you were sorry for your rudeness——"

"Rudeness!"

"Yes!"

She spoke with a certain tone of defiance; her anger blinding her to the fitness of things—he was really but an acquaintance; continued:

"I think so. Tell me, what did you read?"

His silence incensed her more. Tapping her foot impatiently at his manifest reluctance to answer, she went on:

"What does it matter? You say you read the exact opposite of the truth."

"If you insist——"

She was in buckram in a moment; pride stiffened her. Drawing herself up, she interrupted him; spoke with an imperious little gesture:

"Oh, no! I have no right to do that. I merely asked."

Miss Mivvins rose to her feet: a woman's way of terminating an interview. In his sorrow—disappointment—once more he touched her hand restrainingly.

"Please sit down."

The note of pleading sounded in his voice. Then—surely his good angel whispered him which line to strike out—he added:

"Don't go yet. You are right—I was wrong."

CHAPTER VIII

A SOFT GOOD NIGHT

Masters took his stand on that apology and made capital out of it. Miss Mivvins resumed her seat. With all his ignorance of the treatment women expected—out of books—he had acted in strict consonance with the sex's idea of the fitness of things.

To own up to the rightness of the woman you are talking with, and your own wrong, is as oil to machinery. It is an almost infallible way of worming yourself into the woman's good graces; rarely fails. Its lack of truth is compensated for by its success: the Jesuitical theory that the end justifies the means.

"Why I said the exact opposite, was because in your hand there are lines"—he was holding her hand in his now; holding it tightly as if he did not want it to slip away again—"which signify love of admiration—society—entertainment—jewels—riches—luxury—noise—bustle and excitement."

She listened to the catalogue in silence—save for the eloquence of the lashes of her eyes.

"And if," she queried after a moment, "if I confessed to all that—that you had read correctly—what then?"

He smiled, so certain was he of the falsity of his catalogue: that her character was very different from his delineation.

"At the risk of your again calling me rude," he answered, "I should say you were speaking falsely."

"Why?"

"Because in Nature's library there is a more truthful book to read than that of the hand—the face."

She started; he had commenced the perusal of what he referred to. Her slight blush was hidden; a kindly cloud passed over the moon at the moment.

"I have read that face of yours—read it again and again. I read it each time I see you, I read it even when I do not see you; your face is never away from me now."

His voice had grown very soft. Having taken his courage in both hands he made the first real movement in their little comedy. There followed on his speech a slight pause—an interval filled in, as it were, by the provision of accompanying music: the rippling surge.

She essayed to draw her hand away—not putting too much heart in the attempt. He needed to make no superhuman effort to be successful in its retention.

"Do you know that you are the cause of my destruction of three-fourths of a story I have written?"

Her astonishment at his utterance was due to the fact that she did not at all understand him.

"I? Why?"

"The day we met here—a red-letter day in the calendar of my life—when first we sat together on this seat, I was dissatisfied with the heroine I was creating: she was not good enough. You came; I put you in my book; put you in the place of the creation I had been dissatisfied with—the study from life was so much better. And it was so simple; I never had to wander or imagine things about her. She was always—is always—before me."

She persisted in her affected disregard—a poor sort of performance—of the meaning in his voice; asked:

"How have you painted her—me?"

"Unsophisticated, ingenuous, frank, guileless. She comes into the life of a man who has lived away from women, who has never believed in them, never wanted to. She makes the man see the error of his ways; leads him out of the darkness and blackness of his night into the brightness of her day. She becomes his sun."

His words, the manner of their utterance, made her bosom rise and fall. The deep earnestness in his voice would have moved a much harder heart than hers.

"And he?"

His eyes lighted up as, in reply to that question, he began a sort of description of himself.

"He thanks God for the light! Lives! Lives! Sees things in life he never saw before. She has thrown a searchlight on the barrenness of his solitude: shown him its poverty. He realizes that it is not good for man to live alone."

An onlooker just then would have imagined her sole object in life to be the boring of a hole in the tarred path. She was watching her toe at work with an engrossment of the most, apparently, intense kind.

"And all this—these ideas—were born of my—our—chance meetings?"

"Yes! My work became easier; there was no labour. Your face was as a book to me; an open book. I just seemed to copy from it what was written there. But as for chance—who can say? Chance is but unseen direction."

The caress in his voice made itself felt. Ignoring the latter part of his speech she made hurried reply:

"And you read all this in my face? My face which contradicts my hand so?"

So earnest was he, that he grew almost petulant over the wilful misunderstanding, her changing of the subject; said:

"Let the reading of the hand go. I am content with the face."

Looking up, she realized that his eager eyes were fixed earnestly on her. Saw in them the smouldering fire waiting for the smallest draught to lick it into flame.

"Are you reading it now? Don't you know"—with a nervous little laugh— "that it is very rude to stare so?"

He felt reminded of the action of an engine's piston: his heart was pumping so furiously.

"Don't," he urged. "Please don't say so. It would wipe out half the happiness of your presence if——"

That eagerness of his must be checked! There was no knowing how far it would lead! She stepped behind the lattice of conventionality.

"It is growing late." She was on her feet; used the interview terminator again. "We must be returning."

He drew in his breath; was so afraid. Struggled in vain to control his rebellious pulse; fancied he had gone too far. Tried to retrace his steps and found—as most of us do—walking backwards gracefully to be a matter difficult of performance.

"I have not offended you by speaking as I have done, the truth?"

"Offended!"

She spoke shortly. Just repeated his word, not being in a mood for the making of long speeches; added:

"Oh no!... Now let us be going."

They went. Homeward bound the conversation perched on stilts; seemed artificially out of reach; a reserve had sprung up between them. Both were making obvious efforts to be natural. Masters was appreciative of the fact that his own were a sickly failure.

At her gate she assumed merriment; a transparent, fraudulent kind of mirth. Said laughingly, one hand on the latch, the other ready to place in his:

"And now, Mr. Prophet, what of the morrow? Think you will it hail, rain, wind or snow?"

It was not infectious, that merriment of hers. She had fallen on the first subject in Valapuk: the weather. Staple of English intercourse, how many can deny it a debt of gratitude? Common ground—a national heritage whereon we can disport ourselves at ease.

"Rain, I am afraid." He looked round. "Those banks of clouds augur badly."

"You are not a comforting sort of prophet! Assumption of your correctness means confinement to the house all day."

"Yes."

He looked at her as he answered. The glance made it hardly a laconic reply.... She stretched out her hand. With the light in her forget-me-not eyes full on, said:

"Good-bye."

Taking her hand—his retention of it was for a period considerably longer than is considered quite good form in Mayfair—he asked:

"If a wet day—to-morrow, you know—I shall not see you at all, shall I?"

Those eloquent lashes of hers helped her speech as she replied:

"It may clear in the evening, as it did to-day. I may not take Gracie out in the damp. But, unless it rains, I shall take my own walk in the evening."

Even a smaller mercy would have made him thankful. He enquired eagerly:

"At eight o'clock?"

The fringes lifted, giving him what he extravagantly labelled a glimpse of Heaven. In the moonlight he saw all the glory of her eyes, as she answered:

"Yes."

He had never thought it possible that room could be found for so delightful a tone in a woman's voice, as was in Miss Mivvins' utterance of that one-syllable word.

"If you should find me walking on the parade at that time," he suggested, "you—you would not be displeased?"

She looked at him again. What she read prompted her to think him deserving some little reward. Casting her eyes down to her hand, which he was still holding, and lowering her voice too, till it was almost a half-whisper, she said:

"What—what would you think if I said that——"

She hesitated—stopped. Quite eagerly he endeavoured to help her on; interjected:

"Yes?"

"That I might be disappointed if I did not see you?"

The sigh he drew was of a plumbless nature. He answered, his soul in his utterance:

"You will not be disappointed."

The sweetest of sweet tones, speaking in the low, tremulous voice which may say so little but mean so much:

"Good-night!"

A grip of her hand that almost hurt her; a light in his eyes which had never found place there before, and he echoed her final words:

"Good-night!"

Softness in both their voices, in their whole manner. A reciprocated hand pressure.

So they parted.

CHAPTER IX

OVER THE GARDEN WALL

Miss Mivvins was very full of thought of the man who had left her; he was full to the point of over-brimming of thought of her. They were soulful thoughts, which lasted them both till sleep closed the windows of their souls.

In the case of the man the eyelids remained wide open till the grey dawn flushed rosily before the rising sun. Even then he dreamt: of her.

Later, when he awoke, it was evident that a halo of success would surround his weather prophecy. His prediction of wet turned out correct: it rained nearly all day. But Cupid must have bribed Pluvius; the rain ceased to fall as the grey of evening closed down on the day.

Then they met again. It was a walk only; a walk up and down the front. She did not feel equal to trusting herself on that seat again. Did not trust him— or herself.

A moonlight night, a murmuring sea and a man with eyes of greater eloquence than his tongue possessed—decidedly she thought it was best to avoid sitting down.

Miss Mivvins did not altogether seem herself; was nothing like so bright as she had been before. The sweet mouth never parted in laughter once during all the walk. It was a new mood to him; one in which he could find no pleasantness.

He taxed her with it; something was worrying her. He would have liked to plainly ask what, that he might lighten or at least share the trouble. She, not admitting it, endeavoured to shake off the depression.

As their good-byes were uttered, he exhibited a surprising fertility in the invention of hints of meetings again. She, for reasons known to herself, did not take them.

The weather afforded her a shield; she switched the conversation on to that. Clouds were shaping ominously; there was a prospect of more foul weather on the breaking of the morrow. So was avoided any open reference to another evening walk when they parted.

Clouds, of another kind, seemed to envelop him. He had counted so on the meeting; had watched the ticking away of the hours till the fall of eventide: and after, till eight o'clock came.

All the warmth of the previous evening, all his delicious anticipation, was eclipsed by the frigidity of to-night. He felt like one for whom the sun has set while it is yet day.

He worried himself to the point of haggardness: being a man possessed of strong emotions. Walked home mind-laden with fear that he had done or said something to offend her. Racking his brain, yet failed to find a record; could not imagine what had been his sin.

His slumber was not of the peaceful kind. Although his dreams were of her—the woman his waking thoughts were so full of—they were not of the pleasant kind of yesternight. Again, too, he saw the red fringe in the east grow into dawn before he slept.

A warm, drizzling rainy day; so he found the weather on awaking. So warm that at breakfast he had his window open; his landlady referred to the condition of things as being muggy. That was not the only speech of hers he heard that morning.

The proverb about listeners and the good things they hear occurred to him. By reason of the open window he was unable to avoid overhearing a conversation. It was carried on between the next door landlady and his own.

Masters would have scorned a suggestion of eavesdropping. He was aroused from the depths of the morning paper, in the columns of which he was immersed, by hearing his own name spoken. That is usually a call to attention to most of us. The voice of the neighbour reached him:

"Yes. My Liza saw 'em walking together, so to speak. Lord, 'e don't look a gent like that, do 'e? But you never know, do you? As I was only sayin' to Mrs. Robinson this very mornin', quiet ones is always the wust. She's a 'ot lot, and no mistake!"

"Are you sure it was my lodger?"

The inquiry was from his own landlady. He recognized her voice, low pitched as it was: there were top notes in it she could never eliminate. The answer came over the garden wall:

"My Liza ain't a fool, I give you my word! There, as I says, you never know, do you? It don't always do to judge by 'pearances. Your ground floor looks as if butter wouldn't melt in his mouth, as the sayin' is. But she—there! You can tell with 'alf-an-eye what she is."

"Yes. I s'pose there ain't no mistake about that. Fine feathers don't always make fine birds."

"She's going about, in a manner of speaking, plainly dressed too, just now. Ev you noticed it? I see her with my own eyes in Juggins' shop without a single ring on her finger! She as used to ev a 'alf-dozen sparkling di'monds on each 'and."

"Pawned 'em, perhaps."

"No fear! She knows your lodger's well-to-do, and she's working 'im for all 'es wuth, as the sayin' is. Lor! She's up to snuff, I can tell you. As I was sayin' to Mrs. Smith, them kind of women is up to every thing."

A voice, presumably the tones of the afore-mentioned Liza, broke in. The next door neighbour was being called; some one was enquiring about lodgings. The conversation ended with the suddenness of an eye's twinkling.

Little as Masters had heard, he was the whole day trying to digest it. Material for thought was there: a pregnancy of horrible suggestions.

As to his work, he did not write a line; could not read a paragraph. After the manner of a caged beast walked up and down the room. When at last he sat, sheer exhaustion was the compelling force.

His mid-day meal was turned over on his plate; any idea of eating it was out of the question; it was taken away practically untouched. He had no room for physical food; he was so very full just then of mental provender. One dominating thought reigned over all others. What should—what could he do?

His habit was to drink a cup of tea in the early afternoon. His landlady entered bearing a little tray. Whilst she was spreading its contents, the thoughts consuming him found vent. He said:

"Don't go away—for a moment. I want to ask you something."

"Yes, sir?"

"You know Ivy Cottage—on the front? Do you know who lives there?"

She looked at him for a moment before answering. An autumn bird needs careful handling; if it takes flight the nest remains empty till the following summer. She passed her tongue over the thin lips which framed it; said warily:

"No, sir. That is to say, not their present names."

Memory's finger pointed out the conversation of the morning over the garden wall; this woman's share in it. He knew she was lying. His anger against things in general was smouldering; something to let it loose on would be a relief. Why this deceit and mystery?

The wisdom of keeping his foot on the brake was known to him. He was wise enough, too, to grasp the fact that a man in a temper weakens his armour. There was battle to be done; he meant having it out before the woman left his room.

"Is that altogether correct?" he inquired. "Surely you must, living in this place, have heard?"

"Oh!"

Exclamation with a vinegary shake of her head. She was standing now with her mittened hands crossed, prepared evidently for a long talk; continued:

"We hear plenty about them, sir!"

"You know the master of the house?"

"Not the present one, sir—if there is one just now!"

In shaping the deep lines round her mouth his satanic majesty had surely held the graver! Masters thought the meaning smile with which she let loose the innuendo positively hideous in its suggestiveness. His inflammable emotions rendered it difficult for him to get proper control of his voice as he enquired:

"The mistress, then?"

Impatience in the tone of his voice. He had hoped to elicit replies without this direct inquiry. Felt ashamed of himself the while he probed. It was not a feeling the woman shared. She answered:

"Oh, yes, sir."

The readiness of her answer was apparent. She was the kind of woman to whom slander was a dainty morsel to be tongue-rolled. Her own tongue became as the pen of a ready writer. It sickened the questioner, but he continued:

"And the governess?"

Vigorous shaking of the woman's head again. In the same redolent-of-sourness style, too, as she answered:

"There is no governess there, sir. The only servints is the cook and 'ousemaid and the odd boy."

He knew that to be a lie! Hope, that he had thought entombed, rose again. One thing incorrect, why not all? He said sharply:

"You are mistaken!"

"I don't think so, sir."

Again that hideous smile. Accompanied this time by a pitying expression; pity for his simplicity! He was like the generality of men—writhed under pity. It acted on him with the irritation of a rasp. He, however, controlled himself sufficiently to enquire:

"A tall, fair, blue-eyed young lady?"

The description elicited a second edition of the pity—third of the head shaking—as the woman answered:

"That's the mistress, sir."

It is difficult to keep a watchful eye ever on the safety valve. The indignation within him was seething to boiling point. He was getting up steam so rapidly as to create the impression that his emotions were arranged on the principle of the tubular boiler. He blurted out:

"I tell you, you are wrong! Her name is Miss Mivvins!"

Combination of every unpleasant wrinkle that the human face is capable of assuming, as she replied, with the incisiveness of a knife cut:

"Very likely that's one of her names, sir! Now I come to remember, I did once in a shop 'ear her called so—called so by her own child."

That was the last straw! the safety valve was discarded. He blurted out:

"Her—own—child!"

"Yes. The little girl who's always with her. The one with the carity 'air as some people calls orebin."

Amazement! Consternation! Disappointment! A combination of these feelings, and many other indescribable ones, made him break out with:

"Then—then she is married?"

All the subtle devilish suggestions in her came to the surface. To emphasize the point of her answer, slow head-shaking was necessary:

"I couldn't say as to that, sir."

She smiled too that horrible smile again! The desire to speak evil of others assails some natures irresistibly. She really could not resist—October lodger or no lodger.

"Thank you. That will do."

He managed to dismiss her so, and the landlady left the room. She was fearful of having gone a little too far; yet was filled with the complacency with which such utterances—to such natures—is fruitful.

Yes, he was alone—but such a loneliness!

CHAPTER X

THE LITTLE WINGED GOD

The closing of the door behind his landlady was unheard by Masters. He did not move from the position in which the woman had left him for many, very many minutes.

When at last he rose, lifting his head, he caught sight of his own reflection in the mirror. Started back, almost cried out: there was such a deathly pallor covering his face.

His mouth felt as parched as Sahara. Mechanically he mixed a whisky and soda: drank it off. Then laughed. Not a pleasant mirth; one of those built up on a sob.

Then self-raillery: the old, old, ever sought useless salve. What a fool! What a fool he was to care! A woman! Just as he had always pictured them— always till the book he was now engaged on. When he thought how chaste and good and pure his last heroine was, on paper, he laughed again. The same laugh; with the same choking painful little catch-in-the-throat in it too.

He thought he had lost his ideals long ago; we are apt to flatter ourselves so. But their death is hard; they live on—unknown even to ourselves—to appear before us like some new star of whose existence we know nothing. Make it our guiding star, and we are—when it sinks below the horizon of fate—as children crying in the night.

The mantel clock chimed seven times. Masters' attention was thereby drawn to the fact that it was half-past that hour. Lodging-house clocks are not without their peculiarities; the fulfilled ambition of this particular one was to be half-an-hour behind time.

Masters started, too, at the sound. Memory of his neglected work came to him. Lying on his desk was a bundle of corrected galley proofs, which should have been posted to his publisher. Now it was too late: the post bag would be made up.

He was annoyed that he had allowed the incident—he was miserably failing in trying to label it so to himself—to interrupt the routine of his work. Another glance at the clock and he kicked off his slippers and horned on his shoes.

Putting on a cap, fastening his greatcoat as he went, he hurried railway stationwards. For all the thickness of his coat he was not warm. There was a coldness around his heart as if it were icebound.

The last up-train left at eight o'clock. In October the passengers made no great demand on the guard's attention; in the season he might have been, with justness, likened to a sardine packer. Entrustment of the bundle of proofs, to be posted by the railway man on arrival in London, was an easily arranged matter.

Crossing the hand with a piece of silver is as effective with the average guard as it is with a gipsy: the oracle is worked thereby. The proofs would reach the publisher by first post in the morning.

Masters had effected this arrangement by five minutes to eight; five minutes before the scheduled time for the train's departure for London. Having lighted a cigar in the shelter of the waiting-room doorway, he buttoned up his coat, prepared for his return walk home.

As—buttoned up, cigar in mouth—he emerged from the station's precincts, he could not fail to observe the lights in the back windows of Ivy Cottage. The bungalow stood not three minutes' walk away.

That he should have avoided, he knew; but the night was dark; he would not be seen. Moreover, he was in no way different from other moths who ever flutter round candles.

So, more or less unconsciously, he was attracted; slowly walked in the direction of the light. The little god with wings is as experienced in the use of the magnet as the dart.

The corner of the road, which the rear of the house faced, was reached. Suddenly the back door of the house was opened. By the light in the passage behind he saw a man and a woman silhouetted in the door-frame, evidently engaged in actions of a farewell.

The woman had her arms lovingly round the man's neck. She fervently kissed him—his lips—again and again. Her sorrow at the parting was apparently of the deepest kind; at times she applied her handkerchief to her eyes. Not a detail of the incident escaped the attention of the man in the road.

Masters stood quite still watching them. Not an act due to ill-breeding: he was for the moment simply incapable of movement. Had his existence depended on a forward step, Death would have added another name to his list.

The couple came out in the garden; walked towards the gate. The path led straight from the door; the hall lamp still showed him the positions: the woman's arms clinging around the man.

It was well he stood in the shadow on that road; well that they were so occupied as to prevent their noticing him. Perhaps the iron that had entered into his soul travelled viâ his face. That would account for the seared look on it. It was as the face of the dead.

So different. Ah! So different had he thought her. Had linked up, in his mind, the purity of the snow in connexion with her. This was the woman he had pictured; who was ever so before him that his pen seemed animated when he handled it to describe her.

His thoughts—edged with keen bitterness and self-contempt—went back to the pure, guileless heroine in his book. Had he been capable of laughter at himself, for being a fool, his mirth would have been of the greatest heartiness just then.

The couple at the gate parted; the watcher was not very clear how. What followed being—by reason of a sort of indescribable veil or mist which enveloped him—blurred, almost hidden from him. Dazed as was his condition, he was cognizant that the man crossed the road, ran past up the pathway to the station. Then came the sound of a whistle, followed by the rumbling of the departing train.

Footsteps! He knew them—short as had been his acquaintance with them—along the gravel path; then the door of Ivy Cottage was shut. The blackness of the night could not have been heavier than the thoughts he was alone with. Ideas of things seemed to grow more entangled and confused every instant.

From the moment that he had despatched his parcel, he had been mentally accusing himself of folly of the highest class. Did so whilst lighting his cigar and on the way from the booking office—with the back of Ivy Cottage fronting him. Why had he believed those wretched over-the-wall gossips, when there was the face—those soulful eyes—of the woman herself to look into?

That he had listened to and questioned his landlady was an insult to the woman of whom his mind was so full. He knew how those glorious, plumbless blue eyes of hers would flash contempt for him did she but know: she must never know! Standing there—near the house which enshrined what he thought the dearest and best in the world—he almost cursed himself. For his folly in doubting her. His future faith should obliterate the memory of that moment.

Then—then the back door had opened! It was a shock; a horrible shock. But there was confirmation of what he had been told. The scales fell from his eyes.

Minutes—they seemed to him centuries—passed. The mist before his eyes cleared away; the veiling disappeared. But he felt that it would not be a display of wisdom to turn homewards, just yet.

Masters was a sensitive—hyper-sensitive is perhaps a better word—man. To rub up against inquiries from a garrulous landlady as to his health would prove more irritating than sand paper. He knew that his appearance would provoke comment; felt how he looked; determined to try and walk the look off.

By setting his face eastward, continuing on the station road for a mile or so, he would come out on the shore at what was known as The Gap. By walking along the sands therefrom, past the private owner's wall, he would be able to mount to the parade by the steps which faced his seat.

Lips tightened and his fingers clenched when he remembered the reference to this as "our" seat. The walk would do him good; he laughed a little at that last idea. As if, he thought, anything in the whole world would ever do him any good again!

Shaken faith is a wound that smarts acutely; the only surgeon able to apply a salve is Time.

CHAPTER XI

THE VOICE IN THE DARKNESS

It was a fitful night; one on which the clouds travelled swiftly. One moment the brightness of a silvering moon; the next comparative darkness. When the extinguishers hid the lamp of night, the illumination of the heavens was left to the stars.

There was sufficient light for Masters to find his way over the breakwaters without stumbling. At times, though, despite the brightness of the moon, his eyes saw dimly. With a swiftness bred of anger he knuckled the dimness away, cursing his own irrepressible folly the while.

His heart—soul—was full to bursting point. If he could only laugh, he thought; only laugh at himself! What an immense, great big thing it would be!

Walking, smart walking, was the only relief he experienced; physical exertion was reputedly an antidote to mental excitement. He felt sufficient energy to have moved on indefinitely. Wished he could walk on till he fell from exhaustion. In that there would have been satisfaction; rest, at any rate. Rest from that tumultuous tide of recrimination surging in his brain.

His anger was directed against himself; no one else. It upsprung from the fact that he had been such a fool, such an utter, absolute fool, as to be gulled by a woman! Scoffingly he told himself that anger against her would be unfair; that her behaviour had been merely typical of her sex!

He, who had ever with his pen written against womankind—until at last reviewers had spoken of his work as being that of a woman-hater—to have fallen such an easy victim to the first siren who spread her snare for him! The thought was fuel to the maddening fever in possession of him.

Then came before him her face; those sweet, eloquent, soulful eyes! Well, he endeavoured to comfort himself with the thought that any man would have fallen a victim as he had done. The amount of comfort in it, though, would have found resting-place on a needle's point.

There was an underlying reason for the failure. Granted that his ideal was shattered, he still loved its ruins. Therein lay the hopelessness of it all—and he knew it. Striding on, he savagely kicked out of his way, now and then, a stone. Poor sort of relief again.

The configuration of the coast line brought him to an abrupt standstill. The cliff, jutting out, was met by a barrier of high rocks. These latter were overgrown with seaweed of the slipperiest sort: defiance bidding. Nature's sudden intervention in his proceedings produced a corresponding interruption in his thoughts.

Why should he think about this woman any longer? She was not worth wasting thought over. He had been happy enough without her—before he knew her. So he would be happy without her still.

Cut the thought of her clean out of his mind; out of his heart. That, he told himself, was the correct thing to do. Life should be for him as if he had never seen her, never looked into the unfathomable depths of those forget-me-not eyes. It would be quite easy; a little effort of will was needed—that was all.

All that he meant; every word of it. Framed a resolution that he looked on as adamantine. But he ignored an important factor; made no allowance for the strange vitality of that prolific pure white flower: Love.

The axe of common sense may be laid to the root of the tree; may cut it down root and branch. Still one small remaining tendril, hidden from the sight, will work its way into the heart; spread and grow until in its magnitude it overshadows every other thought. Such is love.

Masters reached the steps which led up from the sands to the seat. Standing at their base, he looked away in the direction of the sea. It was easy to mark the spot where Gracie had worked so hard with spade and pail.

He thought of the child with a pang of pity. For his heart had gone out to her; he had been captivated by her loving, winsome ways. Even now his eyes rested on where Gracie had built her last castle. He could mentally see her gleesomely watching the waters overflowing the moat and gradually sweeping down the castle's inverted pail-shaped turrets.

Gracie! Poor little soul! And so she, whom he had mistaken for the governess—this woman—was the mother of that incarnation of innocence and purity! What of the child's future? He shuddered to think of it; it was horrible; all horrible in the extreme.

Well, he would go home to his lodgings. First he would look again—for the last time—on that portion of the sands. For he felt that he would never be able to come there again. He would have been thankful for a breeze just then: his brow was feeling so fevered.

Perhaps there was more air on the seawall; he would test it, pass up the steps. There was the seat to avoid looking at; the seat whereon they had both sat reading—heart reading heart. Where had been born to him the happiest moment in life: love's awakening.

There was other history about the seat too: pencil created. Thereon, before that meeting, had been born heroes and heroines, wicked men and wicked women. All to be bound together and pressed between covers later on, to gladden or sadden readers' hearts.

Living a romance is less alluring than writing one: Masters found it so. He had been wont to believe in the parts he cast his characters for. He was learning!

Stumbling up the steps on to the wall, he started to walk home. But he halted, suddenly, before he had taken half-a-dozen paces. No drill sergeant's command ever brought up an absent-minded beggar on parade as did the words which fell on his ear.

"I thought that was you, Mr. Masters!"

Her voice! The voice of his shattered idol! The same voice: just as fresh and soft and kind as ever! Her voice, speaking to him! Could it be? Or was it a dream simply, a chimera of his brain? Or was this voice—this voice ringing, singing in his ears now—the result of his highly fevered imagination only?

He feared to turn his head to see. To know whether it was in reality the woman for whom he had been ready to lay down his life—whom he had considered a princess among women; chaste, pure, modest; whose dethronation had been so recent. Whom he had come to think of as soiled.

Yes! She was there before him in the flesh! This perfidious parody of perfection, this transmuted ideal. He waited for a moment motionless; then raised his cap—a merely mechanical act.

Besides, being a woman, whatever else she might be, she was exempt from rudeness at his hands.

Her sex protected her.

CHAPTER XII

MISUNDERSTANDINGS

"Aren't you going to sit on Our Seat? Or don't you need a rest?"

It was said archly; the significant reference to Our Seat, subtly conveyed. She seemed to have shaken off the depression of yesterday. Was herself; her own blithe, bright self again.

Mechanically Masters accepted the implied invitation; sat. There ensued silence; a silence which told more than speech. Not the silence which breathes of sweet accord between two understanding hearts.

She, on her part, was filled with wonder—expectancy—an undefined sense of something being wrong. He was not insensible of the fact that the plumage of his dove was rustling. No woman could, of course, endure such treatment.

The need for speech on his part was plain: but, somehow, he was at a loss for words. Was yet alive to the fact that she would read his speechlessness her own way: would set him down as guilty of caddish behaviour. The silence became tense: the strain was fast becoming unbearable.

But little time passed; she got to her feet—being the kind of woman quick to take offence. The insult was felt the more acutely because, she told herself, she was alone to blame: had simply courted it, brought it on herself.

She had wanted to meet this man. Had hurried on to the parade with the feeling in her heart that it would be good to meet him. Had sat on the seat for a minute's rest and a faint sense of grief that she had not encountered him on her walk. Had been thinking disconsolately of walking home, when she was rendered joyful by his presence.

And then—to be treated like that! Had she offended him? Such a possibility passed rapidly through her mind; was as rapidly rejected as a theory untenable. Did he disapprove of her coming there alone, at that time?

She knew that some men were punctilious in regard to such matters. But he—natural, unconventional as he was himself—surely it could not be that. His voice interrupted her reflections. In a husky, strained tone, looking neither right nor left, but aimlessly in front of him, he said:

"Nice, fine evening, isn't it?"

Another credit note to our fickle climate! But the utter incongruity of the remark, the exceedingly strange tone of his voice, caused her to wheel round and look at him. Then she saw. The moon chanced to be free from clouds just then; its pale beams accentuated the lividity of Masters' face.

"Oh, my God! you are ill! What has happened—an accident? What can I do for you?"

As she was quick of thought so she was quick of movement. In a moment was kneeling beside him—all the annoyance and hastily-aroused temper gone to the winds. Only her helpful woman's instinct aching to be of service to him: to the man she loved.

"It is nothing. Don't—please. Don't worry yourself."

Impulsively her arms went up to his shoulders in sheer sympathy and kindliness. All the stiffness, all the resentment, left her. She was only just plainly and simply a woman.

That being the case, her womanly pride was relegated to a back seat. Her precious dignity went down in value; right down to nil. It was not in the question at all—that question she asked as she gave herself to the needs of the moment; asked with real anxiety:

"Tell me—what to do?"

The light was there on her face, in her eyes! Oh, unmistakably there! The light which yesterday he had prayed he might see; that he had yearned for with his heart and soul. Her soft beautiful radiant eyes were looking with eager, tearful anxiety into his own.

For a moment—the influence of the moment and forgetfulness in combination—he felt that he must grasp, grip, strain her to him. Hold her in one long, lasting embrace. Then—he remembered! That an hour back she had been clinging to, looking into another man's face with the same tearful eyes! Oh, the excellence, super-excellence, of her acting! He would have given a king's ransom for the ability to laugh just then—at himself.

Could it be—could it? For a brief instant he doubted. The next moment blamed himself for being a fool. But not a blind fool—oh, no! He had the evidence of his own eyes: the evidence for the prosecution.

Most of us, under such circumstances, willingly take upon ourselves the threefold responsibility of witness, jury and judge. It is instinctive in most men: the desire to ladle out justice. But the appeal court sometimes oversets the decisions; Justice is not infallible—perhaps her blindness has something to do with it.

Few of us betray modesty when wearing the ermine. The more rigorously we silence the opposing counsel—the evidence of our own hearts—the more we pride ourselves on our impartiality, our exemplary Roman-fatherly administration of justice. We are apt to ignore any talk of a Court of Appeal; arrogate to ourselves supreme wisdom.

Curiously enough, the more severe the sentence we pronounce, the more we rise in our own estimation. The rise may not be permanent—seldom is; but while we are at the high water mark of self-assurance we generally make the most of the tide. The sailing along on it is helped by the wind of serene self-complacency; we sun ourselves in vanity of our prowess. Forgetfulness is there; that the tide—like the proverbial lane or worm—has a knack of turning.

The dominant note in Masters at the moment was anger. That such a woman should have power over men. He mentally thanked God that her power over him was of the past. Laid the flattering unction to his soul that perhaps he was cleaner-minded than his fellows. Man applies curious ointments to his wounds!

But that thankfulness did not arrest his anger; made it the greater perhaps. He was hardly in a state of that judicial calm which should characterize dispassionate inquiry. Being angry, he spoke—after the manner of the angry man—foolishly; said brutally:

"This has been a busy evening with you. Don't you get tired of hugging men? I am the second in one hour."

For a moment she made no movement, no sound—save of the quick indrawing of her breath. It was as if some icy blast had suddenly assailed and frozen her to the spot. Her face retained the same look; she was too amazed—not understanding—too astonished to do more than look. He went on mercilessly:

"I saw the parting at your back door; I was passing. Saw you slobbering over a man there as you seem inclined to slobber over me."

It was as if he had struck her! She drew in her breath so that it sounded whistle-like. Fell back; extending her arms, seemed as if she would push him from her as something unclean. In colourlessness her face rivalled his.

"How dare you——"

Those words were shaped on her white lips. Then she stopped. The lips trembled, tightened. Rising to her feet, the indignation in her eyes as she looked down at him completed the sentence.

He laughed; that laugh with the underlying sobbing catch in it, for his laughter was not born of merriment. Said, righteous indignation shining in his own eyes too:

"Dare! What do you mean? The witnessing of it, or telling you of it?"

She scorned reply; he was really too contemptible! Yet the woman in her bubbled to the surface; she could not resist an effort to hurt him:

"And you—you played the spy!"

A raising of his shoulders, a lowering of his eyes, as he answered:

"Call it so if you wish."

He really did not care what she thought of him; plainly showed that. The indifference roused her; she tried again. Spoke with forced quietness— standing a little way from him—her voice full of contempt:

"There is a man bearing your name in the High Street: a blacksmith. I could understand such behaviour on his part. But—a—gentleman!"

Her satisfaction came then: she had hurt. A deep flush streamed over his face, then faded altogether away, except for two red streaks.

"Am I not behaving as one?"

Keenly sensitive to her rebuke, he spoke half-apologetically. The bitterness of the incident was making him more himself. Brought home to him, forcefully, the irony of things.

"Pray pardon me." He rose and stepped towards her. "Will you allow me to see you home?"

"Don't touch me!"

There seemed an absolute fire burning in her eyes, so intense was her scorn. She could not have shrunk from him, or found him more repellent, had he been a leper. Her eyes seemed to scorch him.

He knew himself to be in the right; knew it perfectly well; beyond the shadow of a doubt. But standing before that searing indignation, it was he who appeared to be in the wrong, even to himself—his inmost self.

Such treatment hurt. Thought of the gross unfairness of it too was positively stinging. He who was suffering—the victim—to be put in the wrong! To be arraigned by the victimiser!

His blood, his forehead, seemed to be burning hot, the while he was conscious of cold shivers running through him. Was this—he despised himself as he questioned—carrying out his intention? Was he plucking up his love by the roots?

It was weakness—he labelled it so—weakness on his part that her words, her presence, had still such power to move him. He would be strong—strong and just. But he realized the hardness of the task he set himself. It was man's work; he would prove himself worthy of it.

She did not deign him another word; the wound to her pride was too severe for that. Her blue eyes blazed, as perhaps only blue eyes can. She would have given worlds for tears to soften their burning heat, but no tears came. Without another glance at him she turned and walked away—assumed an every-day gait; he should not think she was excited.

He did not attempt to stop her. Why should he? It was better so. Better that the sharp severing blow had been struck then than later: clean cuts heal quickest. He would let her get well on her way home before he moved. She must not think he was trying to follow.

Standing on the edge of the wall he looked out to sea. The water wore an appearance   of invitation: that dangerous aspect which has proved irresistibly attractive to so many. Right out too, it looked so—so—so away from everything.

The tide was receding; was going out and away—to the Great Beyond. He knew that if he chose he could go with it. It would be so easy an act, if he stepped off the rocks further down—into the water that was always deep.

Then he pulled himself up with a jerk. Pride came to the rescue. Was he to cave in, go under, just because of a woman? What a fool he was! What an unmitigated, arrant fool! Was there a woman in the world—the whole world—worth caring so much for? No. Not one!

But his heart contradicted. He remembered that anxious look on her face, the loving attitude, the feel of her arms as they rested on his breast, his shoulders. His, too, was the remembrance of the warmth of the sweet human breath; her eyes that had looked into his. Then he looked out to sea again; mentally out to the Great Beyond. Asked himself the old, old question: Was life worth living?

Bathos saved the situation. He remembered that a character in one of his stories had asked the same question: Was life worth living? The comic doctor had replied that it depended—depended on the liver!

He walked home.

CHAPTER XIII

FEVERISH SYMPTOMS

Masters did not leave Wivernsea. The obstinacy of his character came into play there; he had come down for a month, and he stopped.

He had come for a purpose too—business purpose—had his book to finish. Was a trifling incident, the accident common to men's lives, to disturb the current of his life? To turn him from his prearranged plan in the smallest degree? Perish the thought!

All he altered was the direction of his walks; he thought that wisdom. Because, like other wise men, he left the east and went west. It was Cliffland there; sheltered spots innumerable were easily found.

She, yet more proud than he, altered nothing; took her walks with Gracie as usual. Sat on the seat at the far end of the walk; read novels there with stoic fortitude—except for an occasional long look across the waters.

Looking across the wide sea seems to afford scope for, to encourage, limitless, aimless reflections. At any rate hers were aimless; she knew that. But a woman dearly loves the memories of the past, to bring them before her: to pet and fondle and keep them alive with the warmth of her heart.

Being at opposite poles, east and west, their daily meetings ended. Once he met her in the post office; he was leaving as she was entering. He raised his hat, and would—from mere courtesy—have said: Good Morning. But the unframed words wilted on his lips.

Her eyes, as they fell on him, lighted up with indignation; a second edition of what he had seen before. As they for a moment rested on him they seemed to scorch up what he would have said. His raised-to-hat hand trembled and fell: he passed out.

Reaching home she found that she had carried with her a recollection of his face. By the seat he had said things to her that no woman could forgive. She told herself that an average hundred times a day—to say nothing of the sleepless nights she passed with thoughts full of him. But she was sorry to see the haggard, worn look he was wearing as he left the post office.

He had appeared ill. His, she had told him, was a face which had borne no worry lines; lines of thought but not of trouble. The absence of the latter had made him appear younger than he really was.

With a smile she thought back on the time—it seemed quite a long while ago—when she had fancied that she had almost come to love that eager, enthusiastic face; boyish, but still with an air of manly determination about it, set in a manly frame.

Masters' shoulders were quite abnormally broad and square; accentuated the impression of strength made by the broad bronzed forehead. How foolish women were, she thought. Well, she had learnt a lesson; she would profit by it. Experience had taught her; she would prove herself a grateful pupil.

She had deceived herself for the first time and the last. Of course it was painful—the awakening. Waking up to the perception of unvarnished facts generally is unpleasant. But she could look at her own foolishness without wincing, indulgently—her foolishness of a week ago. Just an error of judgment that there was no scrap of likelihood of her repeating.

Still—she admitted it to herself—he was undeniably attractive. Hardly less so because he looked older in the post office than he had done formerly. The worry lines, whose absence she had remarked, were there now.

One hasty glance had shown them to her; they were so apparent. She wondered—a kindly feeling stealing over her—whether she had anything to do with it: the change. Then memory came and withered up the softness; pointed out what had been said to her that night when she knelt by the seat! The memory was a blasting breath; her softness fell away.

The mere remembrance of it made her feel hot all over. She—she to kneel to a man! Because she had fancied he was ill—full of kind feelings towards him, she had knelt; and he had talked of hugging and slobbering! To have her kindness, so well meant, recoil on her, thrown back on her hands as it were, with gratuitous, unwarranted insult instead of thanks!

It is galling to have a gift returned; the gall is greater when the gift is of the heart's kindness; more galling still when the ungracious recipient vacates a place in that heart itself. The return then savours of brutality.

Fury, too, came to her at the mere memory of his speech. She was almost as angry as when the words rang freshly in her ears. But with all the temper there was mingled wonder. Surely he could not be a man to whom brutality came easily. Why—why—why—had he behaved so?

Fool? No. She told herself that she was not that. She had read in his eyes that he loved her; indeed, had more than once checked his telling her so. What could be the cause?

He had spoken of seeing her in the back garden that night—but that was a mere incident—there were a thousand-and-one explanations of that. He would know that; there must have been something else.

But why should she worry herself about the matter—about the man? Plainly he was not worthy a second thought. Ready to misjudge her as he had been—well let him! She did not care; not a scrap. She was quite capable of fighting her way alone.

Then she picked up one of the books of his he had given her. On the fly leaf she read:

> *Miss Mivvins; to remind her of Our Seat, on which so many of these pages were written.*
>
> *William Masters.*

She stood with her eyes on the writing, the book in her hand, for many minutes. Then put the volume down with a sigh. After all, she thought, real friends are as rare as Christian charity.

Crunching sounds—boot pressure of gravel, made her look out of the window on to the path leading to the gate. The doctor was coming up it to the house. She went out to meet him.

Gracie was not well—restless and feverish—was now lying on her bed sleeping. The doctor, on his previous visit, had thought it a cold merely, but there were faint symptoms which made him promise to come again. He was there in fulfilment of that promise now.

She was waiting for him at the door when he reached it. Nodding to her, in an informal, friendly way, he questioned cheerily:

"And how is the little one this morning?"

"Much better, I think, doctor. She is sleeping peacefully now."

"Sleeping? Still? Is she drowsy?... Let me see her."

They walked into the bedroom together. The noise of their entrance roused the child. She looked up and around her, with the frightened eyes of one suddenly awakened from alarming dreams.

"Well, little girlie!"

The doctor spoke merrily. He was of that type; did not carry the undertaker with him when visiting a patient. He advanced to take the child's hand lying on the coverlet; continued:

"This is a nice idea of yours, upon my word! Going to sleep in the day——"

His intent in the adoption of a reassuring tone was to change the current of her thoughts: the wild thoughts evidently surging in that active little brain. But when he clasped the child's hand in his own, the merriment left his voice, the smile his face. His other hand he placed on her forehead, then turning, said:

"Why did you not send for me?"

The mother was standing close beside the child, stooping so that her face was on a level with the terror-stricken little one's bright eyes. She was speaking loving words, in the loving way that appeals to children. Words which read so foolishly, yet sound so sweetly. She turned round suddenly, startled by the gravity in the doctor's voice.

"Send!" she cried. "Why? She—she is not—oh, don't tell me——"

"Hush!"

She became quiet at once. Another phase of the doctor's character showed: his will power. The loving anxiety was suppressed. The practical woman was to the fore, intent on the doctor's instructions:

"She must be undressed and put to bed. Have a fire here; it must be kept going night and day. Send one of your maids"—he was writing on a leaf of his note-book as he spoke, and finishing, tore it out—"with this prescription at once."

Gracie was fever-stricken! Tossed in delirium all that night and the next day. All the next day and night—and the mother sat by the bedside, tending, never leaving the little one.

The doctor came three and four times a day. Each time he looked grave. There was no sign of improvement in the child's condition. The mother, worn out with watching, ever looking to him for comfort, read none.

Did ever—during all those hours of wearing, waiting, anxious watching—the thought of Masters cross her mind? She had shut him resolutely out of her heart, turned the key of consciousness upon him. But even bolts and bars are proverbially of small efficacy in such cases.

In those long hours, the only silence breaking sounds were the monotonous ticking of the clock and the short, quick breathing of the little white-robed, white-faced form on the white pillows. Sometimes, then, the woman's resolution broke down; thoughts of The Man crept in upon her all unbidden. Gentler thoughts than she had harboured in the previous days: troubles' softening influence was around.

Their first meeting! She thought of that. Of his affection for Gracie; of the child's love for him. Surely a child's instinctive love and trust went for something. Perhaps, after all—and then those horrible words of his rang in her ears, and she hid her hot face in the white coverlet. Never, never—they were unforgivable. Besides, he did not seek forgiveness.

Strange that, by the bedside of the panting child, with Life and Death fighting for possession of the fragile little form, her ears ever straining to catch the sound of that softer breathing which she knew would signal Life's victory—strange, that with fear and hope surging in her bosom, even while her gentle hand restrained her dear one's restless tossing to and fro and cooled the burning forehead and feverish, clinging little fingers; strange that there should seem no wrong, nothing incongruous in the thought of an almost stranger—of William Masters. Perhaps it was because Gracie loved him so dearly: that must have been the reason.

Poor little Gracie! She little knew what manner of man it was to whom she had offered her affectionate, trusting little heart. Yet he had been kind to her, more than kind. There was pleasantness in the memory of that.

Fugitive thoughts were these; stealing in under cover of the night. Those hours when that watchful keeper of the heart—a woman's pride—is prone to forsake his trust; to leave the secret of that heart revealed before its Maker, and herself. A moment, and the watchful sentinel is back again at his post; repentant for his lapse, guarding his treasure more jealously than ever.

The white soul of the child stood at the entrance of the Valley of the Shadow. Hour by hour the watching woman seemed to see the Shadow deepening, growing. Hour by hour she strove with all the power that in her lay to lead that white soul back into life's sunshine.

The watching and anxiety told on her. The doctor, noting her sunken eyes, had to speak firmly:

"You must take rest. You need it as much as your patient."

"Rest!"

"Don't be foolish! You have a good woman; this woman who is helping you."

"She has been a nurse."

"I see she understands. You must take rest or you will be ill. Ill, too, at a time when you are most needed."

"Tell me, doctor. Oh! For God's sake, tell me—you don't know what she is to me! Tell me——"

"My dear madam, I can tell you nothing. As it nears midnight, will come a crucial time. Humour her; whatever she wants, no matter how extravagant it may seem, let her have it. She has an excitable nature, a nervous temperament. Do all you can to soothe her. She must not worry for anything: it might prove her death. Gratify her desires and she may sleep—sleep will be her salvation. You understand?"

"Yes, doctor."

"Whatever she asks for, gratify her."

"Yes, doctor."

"She is needing sleep; rest for that active little brain of hers. She is full of ideas of triple-headed giants, fairies and stories of that sort. Don't contradict her, get her into a state of contentment if possible. Who is this Prince Charlie she was asking for just now?"

"A friend—a casual friend—some one we know."

"She is inexplainably anxious to see him. Soothe, by letting her do so if possible. She has intervals when she is as rational as you or I; it is well to prolong those by letting her talk to people she knows and wants to see. Does he live far away—this Prince Charlie?"

"In—in the town."

"Then, by all means, if she asks again, send for him."

"Yes, doctor."

"Fretting and excitement are to be avoided. Soothe her in every possible way; gentleness and firmness combined go a long way. But this Prince Charlie—from the hold he seems to have on her—may go a longer way still. Of course she may not ask for him again—maybe it is a mere delirious fancy—but if she does, you will know how to act."

But Gracie did ask again. Asked persistently, petulantly, pleadingly. The watcher with the breaking heart allowed the mother in her nature to smother the mere woman. She resolved to humble herself in the dirt: to send for him; he who had so grossly insulted her.

She would not write, she would not see him herself: she could not. She would send a verbal message. Late as it was there was no fear of not finding him up, she knew. He had told her that he always wrote till one in the morning.

The midnight oil phrase was one he was ever using.

CHAPTER XIV

TO BEG FOR MERCY

An upward glance at the clock on the mantel. It was late: within an hour of midnight. The servants had already gone to bed. Going to their rooms she gently knocked at the door; called to one of them by name:

"Ellen!"

"Yes, ma'am."

The reply in a frightened, startled voice. The tone betrayed the maid's fear that she was to hear bad news. The next words were a relief:

"You know where Mr. Masters lives?"

The possibility of a want of knowledge on the part of the servants never occurred to her. She was not in the least surprised when an affirmative answer was returned to her:

"Yes, ma'am."

"I want you to get up at once, Ellen—I am sure you will not mind—and dress yourself quickly. Go to Mr. Masters, give him my compliments, and ask him—ask him to come here—to be kind enough to come here at once."

"Yes, ma'am. Certainly."

The girl had listened in astonishment, but obediently set about the task set her. She was fond of children, was Ellen; was thankful too that she had not, as she had feared at first, been called to hear bad news about Miss Gracie.

The maid had no thought of grumbling at the late service demanded of her, although greatly wondering at the message she was to deliver. The overwrought, tired woman returned to the sick room and waited. Presently the little lips—for the hundredth time—shaped the question:

"I want Prince Charlie; won't he come and tell me about the fairy and Jack?"

The mother's heart was full of thankfulness that she had sent; that she had humbled herself to do so. She was able to bend over and whisper:

"Yes, darling. Mother has sent for him. He will be here directly."

She was without fear in making the promise; felt so sure he would come. He was a gentleman, he would understand. He would know how urgent must be the need which could demand his presence at that late hour—indeed, to send for him at all. Or would he think—No! The thought was too horrible! She stifled it.

Waiting, waiting, waiting—weary waiting! At last she heard the maid's returning steps on the path without; ran to the door and opened it. The girl spoke reluctantly; what she had to say made the mother turn sick at heart.

"Said, ma'am, it was too late to come out to-night. He would come round in the morning."

The mother's mind failed to grasp it: that message. The callous cruelty of it. It seemed too—too impossible. Had he misunderstood—misjudged her? Could it be? Had she fallen so low in his estimation? A crimson flood overspread her face.... After a pause, as if clutching at a straw, she inquired:

"Did you see him yourself?"

"Yes, ma'am. He seemed to wonder what you could want with him. Said it would keep, whatever it was, till the morning."

"Keep—till—the—morning!"

Gracie's pleading, her own promise, rang in her ears! Keep till the morning. The irony of it! She staggered against the wall, passed her hand across her brow—loath to believe that the author, fond of children, could behave so—asked again—

"You are quite sure you saw him yourself?"

"Oh, yes, ma'am. I know Mr. Masters quite well by sight." She did—Masters, the blacksmith! She had been to his shop in the High Street, and in response to her ringing of his house bell, he had put his head out of his bedroom window and spoken to her. Not in any very pleasant tone; he was not pleased that his beauty sleep had been broken into.

He was an early-to-bed and early-to-rise old man. He could see no sense in turning out at past eleven o'clock at night for any one. Not even for a sick child or for the finest lady in the land.

As he went grumbling back to his bed the blacksmith muttered that some of them fine ladies seemed to think it was a nonner to be at their beck and call; summat to be proud of, it was, for a poor man like hisself. None of their airs for him—he wasn't having any, this time. Such was his grumble; weighted with a plethora of adjectives—of a quite unprintable kind.

The mother staggered back into the bedroom, to the child's side. White-faced, trembling in every limb, supported herself by the bed rail. Noted the hour: past eleven o'clock. The crucial time the doctor had spoken of was approaching.

Gracie was in a quite rational mood. Her brightly burning eyes were fixed on her mother as she entered the room, and she spoke at once, eagerly—as eagerly as the feeble little lips could frame words—stuttering in her eagerness:

"Has Pr—Prince Charlie come yet, mamma?"

Right down into the depths of despair sank the mother's heart. She took the child's hot hand in her own; gently brushed the curls away from the little forehead with the other. As she did so the hot dryness of that brow was brought to her notice afresh. It was necessary to answer the child; the reply was gently given. Yet the utterance of each word was as a stab to her:

"Not—not yet, darling."

A little whimpering, plaintive voice uprose from amongst the pillows:

"I want him, mamma—won't he come?"

How was she to gratify the little one's desire: to get Prince Charlie there? The doctor had warned her that at this stage the child's demands were to be granted if possible. If possible. She had sent and he had refused to come. The doctor's words rang in her ears. If Possible.

She thought of the man sitting—as she knew he would be—shaping with his pen, fictional pathetic pictures, intended to draw tears from the tender-hearted. She thought of the real pathos of this child, perhaps dying, to whom he might bring life and hope by his mere immediate presence. And he had returned the message: That It Would Keep.

The child tossed uneasily from side to side. The corners of the arched little mouth went down threateningly. If Possible! Was it possible to bring him—by any means? Was it possible for her to sink her womanhood even deeper? To humble herself to Beg of him to come? Would he come even if she did?

Then the direction came from the little form tossing restlessly from side to side; the weak voice whispered:

"You said he would come, mamma. Won't you fetch him? He will come if you fetch him."

Would he? Was that the possibility? Was the little one wise in saying that? She remembered that out of the mouths of babes and——Well, she could but try. The mother in her was mighty, stronger than all else: prevailed.

There was no mental balance used in her decision. No conscious weighing of pros and cons. The duty—if aught prompted by love is duty—stood clear before her. Something greater than her own will impelled her decision. She would at once go to him herself.

Glancing at the clock again, she saw that the recorded time was half-past eleven. She would go to him. Go on her knees to him: would not spare herself further. Would beg him, for God's sake, to be more merciful than he had shown himself in his message. Entreat him not to put off till tomorrow—when it might be too late—that which could be done to-night.

Self-blame just then she was very full of; bitterness for not having gone to him in the first instance herself. Tortured herself with the thought that it might now be too late. Wondered if God would forgive her obstinate pride. Still be merciful to her: still let her keep her child.

She bent over the bed and spoke close into the little ear. Made spasmodic but unavailing attempts to control her emotion: could not bring herself to utter the words more than just audibly:

"You'll be quite still, darling, won't you, whilst mother goes to fetch him?"

The face turned upwards. The mother kissed it passionately, tenderly, again and again. The wasted little arms went round her neck and clung there gratefully. Mother was going to fetch Prince Charlie!

From the adjoining room the woman who assisted in the child's nursing came; posted herself by the bedside. Then the mother—staggering as if the unknown gaped before her—left the room. In the hall slipped on the cloak which, she remembered, he had buttoned.

She spent no time in seeking a hat. Swung the hood up from behind over her head. So hurried out of the house.

So, into the night.

CHAPTER XV

ON HER KNEES TO HIM

Wivernsea was asleep. Like its blacksmith, it believed in the theory of early rising. Not a light was to be seen in one of the windows she passed. Not until she came to the end of the Marine Terrace. There she saw an illuminated window: her beacon.

It was but a short distance from her own place; not ten minutes' walk. She seems to have spent as many hours in covering it. Despite the proverb, time does not always fly.

The house which Masters lodged in was known to her. He had described the quaintness of its old-fashioned bay window; the only one in the row. She would have known it as his place without even the beacon light for identification. He was a slave of the lamp: consumed the midnight oil.

As she made towards the light she prayed, almost aloud. Prayed for a conquering power—over her pride. That she might be humble. For the framing of words to move this man when she besought him to come. Soulfully prayed that God would incline his heart to hear her prayer.

Three steps—she faltered up them; proximity to her goal rendered her invertebrate—brought her to the level of the door. If she put her hand over the rails she could tap at the window. It would be better so than disturbing the household by knocking. She tapped.

Her actions elicited no response! She waited, with a hard-beating heart. Still no reply: dead silence! Had he expected this—this visit of hers—and resolved to remain obdurate?

The window blind was not pulled down to its full length. Through the lace edging she could see the man calmly writing; writing as if thoroughly engrossed in his work. Evidently the thought of his cruelty did not trouble him in the least.

In desperation, there seemed nothing else to do, she used her fingers again: loudly. Masters looked up; started in astonishment. Heard a distinct tapping on the glass of his window!

He walked to the casement; pulled the cord attached to a spring roller, and in a moment the blind had shot up. Outside all was moonlight brightness. At first he looked straight away; saw only the sea with the intervening roadway. Then, suddenly, at the side, on the steps, saw a woman with a ghastly white, haggard face looking at him! The Woman He Loved!

Start? He almost jumped in his amazement! Was he dreaming? Was it his phantasy? Then he came plump to earth; lost no further time in surmises; went to the door.

The room opened on to the hall; the street door was but a couple of yards away. He had gripped its handle and opened it in a moment. The woman was there—no phantasy—flesh and blood, clinging to the railings.

"My God! What has happened to bring you at this hour?"

"Just—a—moment!"

The answer given weakly; breathlessly. A swerve, and she would have fallen, but for an almost nerveless clutch at the railings—but that he was by her side in a moment, with a strong upholding arm round her waist.

There was unconsciousness of his clasp; things were all going round with her.... She had a feeling of being lifted; then set down again. Then—then a blankness: consciousness left her.

For a brief moment Masters held her in his arms; her whole weight. For a brief moment the blood coursed wildly through his veins; surged brainwards. A wild, mad impulse seized him: to press his lips to hers, helpless, passive as she lay there.

With difficulty he restrained himself. Laid down his burden reverently; her angel's face seemed eloquent of innocence. Once, surely once on a time, it had spoken truth. Ah! What Might Have Been.

She opened her eyes. Found herself lying on a sofa. Masters standing by her side, holding brandy. She tried, feebly, to push it away; but his now full-of-authority voice commanded:

"Drink!"

She was constrained to do so by reason of a hand which went under and lifted her head; another which placed the glass to her lips.... Struggling to a sitting position, passing her hand across her eyes, with a pitiful little drooping at the corners of her mouth, she said:

"I beg your pardon for—for—Was I silly? Did I—I felt a little faint."

He remained watching her. His own face had grown almost the colour of hers. He had touched her, had had her hand in his, had felt the softness of her hair! It seemed to him as if the noise of the beating of his heart drowned the ticking of the clock.

"Tell me," he inquired, still supporting her, "what brings you here so late?"

She shook her head. Womanlike, answered his question by another:

"Didn't the girl tell you?"

"What girl?" He asked in surprise. "Didn't the girl tell me what?"

"About Gracie. I—I sent to you half-an-hour ago. She—they tell me—I think—Oh, my God!—I am so—so afraid!—is dying. She asked for you again and again. You sent a message that you would come tomorrow."

"I!"

His astonished look, the blaze of suddenly aroused anger in his eyes, frightened her. Could he be even now deceiving her? His kindness—was it falsity? She hurried on with her explanation; in her embarrassment the words tumbled from her lips.

"Yes. You did—did you not? Ah! Don't tell me there was any mistake—the girl saw you herself! I ought to be with Gracie now, but you wouldn't come when I sent for you. She—I—thought if I came for you, you wouldn't be so hard. You could not—oh, you could not—if you knew that perhaps her very life depended on you."

In speaking she had fallen on her knees; knelt to him in her entreaty. It hurt; he could not bear to see her—a woman—in this attitude of supplication to him. Almost roughly he raised her to her feet.

When erect, not seeing through her tear-streaming eyes, choked with her emotion, she plucked at his coat sleeve. The action horrified him; recalled the night he had stood beside his mother's death-bed; the dying woman had plucked at the counterpane in just such a way. Roughly—to hide his aroused emotion—he shook himself free.

Then she seized on and took his hand in her own burning hot shaking ones. Continued to plead, sobs breaking her utterance:

"It is a child; a little child dying! She wanted to see you so much! The doctor said we were to gratify her, soothe her, and perhaps get her to a sleep which will save her life. You will come back with me—oh, you will, will you not? She knows I have come to fetch you. She was so confident you would come! I—I have annoyed you, or done something to displease you, I know that, but I am all humility now, Mr. Masters; humble, oh, so humble!"

She had slid to her knees again before he could stop her; continued;

"Humbly begging your pardon for whatever I have done. Praying you, for my little child's sake, to come back with me, please.... Please.... Please!"

For a second time he stooped and raised the sobbing woman; bodily picked her up. He was naturally a strong man, and the feeling filling him just then lent additional strength.

He was so much moved by the present that he lost sight of all he had heard, all he had seen in the past. Only knew that this woman, whom he loved with all his heart and soul, whose shoes he would have kissed, knelt to him.

"How dare you?"

His question was put fiercely, as in that moment of lifting, he held her tightly to him. He repeated it:

"How dare you kneel to me? How dare you beg of me to do what the most inhuman wretch in the world would do?"

For a moment he left her side; inside that time had slipped into his overcoat and drawn a cap from his pocket.

"Finish that brandy."

There was that in his voice which commanded obedience; she never thought of disobeying.

"You will come?"

She put the question tremblingly; holding the glass to her lips as she did so with a shaking hand.

"At once."

A feeling of anger took possession of him: that she could put such a question; he continued:

"How can you ask?"

Her only answer was a soulful, grateful cry; a cry from her heart:

"Thank God!"

He was feeling himself considerably less of a hero than on the last occasion of their meeting. But this was not a time for thought; as he opened the door he said, speaking almost gruffly:

"You can see your way?"

There was quite light enough shed by the moon for that; and there was light ahead too! She knew she could rely on him; the very sound of his voice told her that; was an inspiration in itself. Making her way to the hall door she staggered out; down the little stone flight to the pavement.

Ere she reached the bottom step, he had turned down the lamp, closed the house door and joined her.

"Take my arm.... Cling to me tightly. You are not fit to walk alone."

And she clung. Forgot all he had said to her. Just had something strong and powerful to cling to in her time of trouble, and she clung. Her heart beat so as to pain her. She heard him speak and spoke to him in reply. But all the while her heart was full of prayers of gratitude. God had been very good to her.

Every step they took brought them nearer the bungalow. Nearer the realization of hopes upon which she had almost erected a monument. She knew—felt rather—for certain that he would save Gracie. Faith was strong in her.

He kept her talking all the way they walked. Thought to divert her mind from thoughts of the sick chamber they were coming to. But she wanted to think of it; there was happiness in the thought. Her companion's voice rang so cheerily—it gave her hope. There seemed magic in it; power to dispel doubts and fears.

"What did you mean by a girl and a message you sent half-an-hour ago? My landlady went to bed about nine o'clock. There has not been a soul near the house since."

"A mistake evidently."

She answered feebly. Was too fatigued to seek explanation. He was there, going home with her—that was enough.

"In some way, yes. But there was no mistake in your thinking me capable of such brutality as——"

He stopped. Recollected the words he had himself used to her in his anger at their last meeting. She was entitled to judge him so; was fully justified. The reflection was bitter as gall.

She had no suspicion why he paused. Had she known, her answer might have been different. As it was she said meekly:

"Please don't be angry with me."

It would have been impossible for her to choose words more likely to touch him in his present mood of self-reproach. She spoke too with such an appeal in her tremulous voice, that retention of his anger would have meant changing his whole nature.

He strode on. It was all she could do to keep up with him. His anxiety was to get where he might be of help. He forgot; he had had so little to do with women.

They reached the bungalow. Divested themselves of their outdoor garments in the hall. The house was so quiet, Death himself might have been in possession. It struck an unpleasant chill to the new comer.

Then he followed her to the sick room.

CHAPTER XVI

GOD'S LITTLE BOY

Gracie was sitting up in bed, propped up by the pillows. Masters gave a sigh of relief: they were not too late. Death might be knocking at the door, but had not yet been admitted.

The child looked expectantly at the door as her mother opened it. Her cheeks and eyes were bright with the fever in them. Then the expectant look mellowed into a smile. She had seen the man behind!

"I knew you would come, Prince Charlie!"

"Of course you did! Knew I should come when I knew you wanted me. I shouldn't have been much of a Prince Charlie if I hadn't, should I?"

Masters sat on the bed with his back against the headrail. Put his arm round the little one and snuggled her to him. She nestled up to him with a croon—a little grunting ejaculation of content—as he tucked the clothes closely round her. Did not seem to desire to talk, was just simply happy in having him there. He inquired:

"Comfy?"

"Awful."

He was grieved to feel how she had fallen away. How, in a few days, she had grown so thin. For the mother's and child's sakes, he made no outward manifestation of his grief: expressed no surprise. He felt that his mission just then was to brighten, not to shed gloom. Spoke jestingly:

"Now that Prince Charlie is here, what have you to say to his royal highness? Nothing?"

"I dreamed a dream, Prince Charlie!"

"Oh!"

"Yes. That you were married to me; that you were my husband."

"Did you? Now that was something like a dream! What sort of husband did I make?"

"I don't know. You see the dream didn't last long enough."

"That was a bad job! Because if you had liked me in the dream, you might have married me later on."

"I thought that." She spoke quite gravely. "But you see I know I should like you as a husband."

"I am glad you think that."

"Who asks? Do you say to me 'marry me,' or do I say to you 'marry me'?"

"M'well, that depends. I really don't think it would matter much; which ever way you like best."

"Of course, you would marry me if I asked you? What do I have to do—kneel down, like the Prince in Cinderella?"

"That is the really proper way, of course. But if you have a very pretty pinafore on it would be a pity, wouldn't it? Then I think you could manage without kneeling."

"I see. I could put on my black dress, though. It's got some sticky stuff I spilt down the front."

"But I am afraid before this marriage takes place you will have to grow a little older."

"Of course!"

She essayed a laugh. The mother pricked up her ears: it was the first time the sound of laughter had come from those lips for many an hour; the child continued:

"You don't think I am so silly as to think I can be married in short frocks, do you? What an old goose you are! Of course, I mean when I am bigger and wear a train."

"I see. Do you think the black dress will grow too?"

"N—no. I forgot that—that's my fault. But you promised."

"Why certainly. I most cheerfully promise that I will marry you, if you ask me when you are a big girl."

"A real, real promise?"

"A most really, real, realiest of real promises. If you ask me when you are a big girl, to marry you, I promise you I will."

She sighed contentedly. Nestling to him, closed her eyelids as she said:

"People go away for honey-dews, don't they?"

He smiled. Gathered that she had confused names by reading the label on his tobacco packet. She had seen him fill his pouch, and clamoured for the silver paper to make impressions of coins on. To her huge satisfaction had more than once induced him to pick up her coinage in the belief that they were real.

"Yes," he answered. "It is usual for married persons to go away. We must consider where we will spend our honeymoon. You have been to the Hippodrome, haven't you?"

Her eyes opened; sparkled at the recollection. The dustmen were banished for a moment as she answered:

"Twice! That's where I saw Cinderella!"

"That wouldn't be altogether a bad place for a honeymoon, would it? Then there's the Zoo—how about that?"

"Lovely! You are a very dear old Prince Charlie. I think if I couldn't marry you I wouldn't marry anybody. I am sorry for all the other little girls that can't marry you. You know lots of little girls, don't you?"

"Yes. But then you are my real sweetheart, you know."

"I'm glad. 'Cos you can't marry more than one, can you? I hope the other little girls won't cry, all the same."

"I don't think they will. Some of them are bigger than you; have given up crying."

"Oh, big little girls cry! But they don't make a noise, and they don't like you to see. I've seen mamma cry!"

Prince Charlie was silent; he too had seen the mother's tears. The child prattled on:

"We shall have to go all the way to Heaven when we are married, shan't we?"

He wondered what childish idea could prompt such a question; asked:

"What makes you think that, darling?"

"When we went to church last Sunday—no, it was the Sunday before; the man in the white dress said so."

"Did he?"

"Yes; he did really. I heard him quite plainly. He said 'marriages are made in heaven.' Is heaven very, very beautiful, Prince Charlie?"

"Much more beautiful than we can even think it is, darling."

"All the good little girls go there, don't they?"

"Yes. Most certainly."

"When doctors come to people they are ill, aren't they? And they die sometimes when they are ill, don't they?... If I die now shall I go right straight to heaven, Prince Charlie?"

The woman kneeling by the bedside turned away her head. The trembling hand found her throat and helped to stifle the sob bursting there. Life and death were fighting for conquest. Contemplation of the battle is ever sad; sadder because the watchers can do nought to turn the tide of victory. Time was arbiter; yet the little one was speaking as if the Grim One's victory were assured.

There was a little quaver, just a little huskiness, in Masters' voice, as he said:

"Don't talk of dying, Gracie."

"Oh, I am not going to die yet."

The child's attempt at a laugh was pitiful, by reason of the lack of mirth in it; she continued:

"I shouldn't be able to marry you till you got to heaven if I did, should I? How full it must be up there of little boys and girls, Prince Charlie."

"Yes, darling."

He acquiesced aloud; truthfully. Then added, under his breath:

"Of such is the Kingdom of Heaven."

"God is very fond of children, isn't He?"

"Very fond."

Again there came to him a suggestion; to himself he quoted:

"Suffer little children to come unto Me."

"You are very fond of little children too, aren't you?" She nestled, if possible, a little closer. "Mamma says she knows you are."

"Mamma is right, darling. Very fond."

"But you don't love any of them better than you do me, do you?"

Her blue eyes were fixed on his face as she looked up, eager to hear his reply; quite truthfully he answered:

"Not one. Not one."

"I forgot." A little sigh of content. "You told me that before. You haven't any children of your real own, have you?"

"No dear."

"I'm glad of that."

She sighed in the same way again. Pillowed her head more deeply on his arm; inquired suddenly:

"God has a Child of his real own, hasn't He?"

"Yes, love."

"A little boy?"

"Was a little boy; yes, darling."

"I know. Because we keep His birthday; same as we keep mine. Only mine comes with the roses, His with the holly. You know—it is on Christmas day."

"Yes; we all of us keep it, dear."

"Prince Charlie?"

"Yes, darling?"

"Do you know any stories about God's Little Boy?"

"Yes, dear; some."

"Tell me—a nice story about Him—will you? No giants or bears in it, because I feel so sleepy—and I am too tired.... So tired.... I would like to go to sleep—just like this—in your arms."

He bent his head. Kissed the flushed, sweet little face he was cradling in the hollow of his arm. Then told the story of the birth of God's Little Boy; in a manner adapted to the little ears listening to it.

Her sleepiness grew; the blue eyes opened each time more reluctantly. As the little body lost its stiffness, he blue-pencilled the story down to the stage where God's Little Boy was lying asleep in the manger. And the watching angels—even as the narrator was—were continually saying:

"Hus-s-h!"

The fact that he repeated this part of the story again and again to bring in the soothing "Hus-s-sh" passed unnoticed by Gracie. Her eyes had closed; she was asleep. The doctor had said sleep would be her salvation.

The crucial time—midnight—and she slept!

CHAPTER XVII

THE PASSING OF THE NIGHT

The tone of the story-teller's voice had grown softer and softer; had dropped lower and lower; then stopped altogether.

The silence caused the woman, whose pent-up emotion had been finding vent in silent tears, to uplift her head. Her very soul was gladdened by the picture upon which her eyes rested.

The man had drawn the coverlet up so that it shielded the wearied little eyes from the light. Her child was asleep! Peacefully sleeping in the arms of Prince Charlie.

She had been kneeling with her face buried in her hands, on the same side of the bed as he sat. Now she had but to bend to reach his disengaged hand. The burning, feverish lips were pressed to it, with all the heartfelt fervour inspired by a mother's gratitude: surely the very strongest inspiration in the world.

Ere she took her lips away he felt, drop—drop—drop. Three tears on his hand! Tears from the eyes of the woman to whom, in her grief, his heart opened. Despite the fact that he had thought it closed against her for ever.

His heart was very full just then. A veritable agony of love was in his eyes as he looked at her. Passionate words were framed in his thoughts; rose to his lips and were choked back.

Except for that strained expression in his eyes, his face was calm as stone; the pallor likened it to marble. But the woman's head was bent; his suffering was unseen by her.

It pained him—her gratitude. He had done so little to deserve it. Indeed would have been a brute had he done less. No thanks were due to him; acceptance of them made him feel himself in a false position. But he could do nothing to restrain her—for fear of waking Gracie.

She moved a little away, glancing again at the sleeping child with a deep sigh of thankfulness. A slight movement of his head, a look in his eyes, beckoned her to come closer.

She understood. Noiselessly walked behind him; stood so, leaning over the bed rail. Her head was close to his, as he asked in an undertone:

"The medicine?"

"She should take it in two hours."

"She must."

He said that in a whisper, with a meaning glance at the child's flushed face.

"Will it be wise to awaken her?"

"Distinctly; in case of fever. Besides, at this stage, the more she sleeps the more easily she will go to sleep again. Poor little mite! This is not half so comfortable a position for her as if she were lying down, but I can't move her till the slumber feeling gets a tighter hold on her. I shall awaken her at medicine time, and she will go to sleep quickly enough by then in any position. Drink?"

"Milk. There is some."

She pointed to a jug standing on a table near by. His eyes followed the direction of her hand; he nodded.

"Good. Now, lie you down on the sofa. Try and get some sleep yourself."

She drew back in astonishment at his suggestion. Shook her head; then expostulated:

"I could not!"

"You must!"

"I cou—"

"You don't want to annoy—to seriously annoy me, do you?"

The voice was very earnest; that voice which she found so wonderfully deep and thrilling. Even in its whisper there was, for her, all the power of great music; even in the lightest words he spoke.

She brushed a tear from her eyes. Once more impulsively bent and kissed the hand which was resting on the rail. He whispered:

"Let me ask you to lie down—to oblige me. Will you do that? You have not slept for long. I, as you know, am a veritable owl; a complete night-bird. My consumption of midnight oil is a standing joke. It is easier for me to keep awake than to go to sleep—oblige me."

All the boy in him had departed for the time. Yet there was no effort, no conscious assumption of manly dignity. On the contrary, it suited him well. Seemed merely another phase of his character.

Her answer was in as earnest a tone as he himself used; strangely earnest considering the smallness of his request; she said:

"I would do anything—anything in the world you asked me."

"Then lie down. Remember that the greatest pleasure you can give me will be to see you asleep. That is not very complimentary to you, is it?"

That was said in an endeavour to make her smile. He was sorry he had spoken so when he saw how the lips curved. Sad smiles are not pretty things; he continued hastily:

"And you may sleep in peace. Your fears may be at rest; Gracie is doing well. Short as has been her sleep, so far, I feel the temperature is lower—her breathing to be more regular. Now go."

Dutifully, obediently, she went. There are some men who must be obeyed without question. Masters was of those—when he chose. That was not often. He was of so kindly a nature that he never cared to press his authority: unless occasion rendered that course absolutely necessary.

The sofa was on the other side of the room. He furtively watched her for a long time, as she lay there with her eyes wide open. Watched her unavailing fight against sleep; smiled when at last she succumbed, when Nature conquered. She went to sleep: a sound sleep bred of that previous wakefulness and anxiety.

Time passed. The hands of the clock on the mantel crept round slowly minute by minute, twice. Then, very quietly, very gently, he woke the child. She was so sleepy and drowsy that his heart smote him; it seemed almost cruel to rouse her.

The eyes opened widely for a minute in surprise at seeing him there. Then she remembered; the lids half closed again. She stretched her hand a little higher up his shoulder and said:

"You're still here, Prince Charlie."

"Yes, darling. I am going to stop all night. We must not speak loudly; Mamma is asleep; and she is so tired."

"So am I, Prince Charlie. Peepy and thirsty. Will you give me some milk?"

"After this medicine, dear.... There. Now the milk.... My! What a thirsty little girlie. What? More!... We shall have to buy another cow!"

He smoothed her pillow, laid her comfortably down and stroked her brow. Was glad to note how fast the feverishness was leaving her; she was distinctly cooler. In less than a minute she was peacefully asleep again.

A good nurse, was Masters. Many trained to the calling might have taken hints from him. Some men are born that way.

He had in his composition just the right proportions of firmness, kindness, and that constant thoughtfulness for others which go to make up the ideal attendant.

Moreover, he had a way, through some subtle influence of his personality, of making his will felt without irritating by its actual expression. He rarely raised opposition; rather it fell away before him.

Gracie was not the only being who succumbed to this man's latent force of character. Most people with whom he came in contact felt its power, wholly unaware of it as he was himself.

Yet another satisfied glance at the sleeping figure, then he made preparations for the night. Quietly drawing off his boots, walked across the room to the fireplace. Converted his fingers into tongs, and so from the coalbox noiselessly replenished the fire. Then he sat down to watch; to watch and think.

For hours he sat there without stirring. Made no movement lest he should disturb the sleepers. He was over-anxious perhaps—afraid to make the smallest sound.

His reflections were not altogether in the groove they had followed hitherto. He had felt certainty where now he felt doubt. There were, too, throbbing moments when he doubted not the woman, but himself.

But ever the truth, the bitter truth, rose up before him, like a great black veil. In it was no loophole for charity. Besides, love asks for love—not for compassion. Could she know what was in his mind, she would scornfully refuse his pity. He knew that; had no doubt of it, low as he deemed her to have fallen.

She would reject so poor a substitute for love, and she would be right. There would be no hesitation; he knew that instinctively. He had once seen the blaze of anger in those now closed eyes; the memory remained with him. Yet that substitute was all he had to offer her; all he felt for her now—so he told himself.

Was it? Was it in very truth? He asked himself the question, and his throbbing heart made answer. But his lips formed another reply, although unspoken. They were tightly shut, firmly set. The tenseness was the reply itself.

Yet—he could not help it—he wondered whether it could be possible. That the woman, from whose face he scarcely took his eyes, was what he thought her. Whose emotion and love for her child had been so real and earnest, whose gratitude had shown itself in her humility to him. To him! He who had so grossly insulted her that night on the seat.

Even in sleep, tell-tale sleep, when that watchful control which we may keep on our waking expression is no longer possible, even then the lines of her face were all of purity and gentleness.

The lips were closed in sweet soft curves; a faint flush was on her pale cheeks; her white brow was wholly serene. It was surely as innocent a face as the little one's to which—he saw it now for the first time—it bore so striking a likeness. Was it possible that a woman could sin, or be sinned against, and remain unsullied?

When the time for medicine came round again, he gently touched the child with intent to waken her. Then drew away his hand. He felt that she was so much cooler, the flush had almost gone from her face, that he determined not to disturb her. To let her awaken of her own accord.... So the night passed.

During all those long hours, Masters might have applied wisdom to a grasping of the situation. But it has been well said that wisdom does not pour knowledge from above as the clouds let down rain. It is to be delved for patiently and with hard toil, at the cost of flinty hands and, mayhap, of skinned knuckles.

CHAPTER XVIII

THE BREAKING OF THE DAY

The eastern sky was painted rosier and rosier; day broke. Still the sleepers slept, and the watcher watched. Never moved he except when need arose to feed the fire.

Seven o'clock. Eight o'clock. Then Gracie woke. Gracie, save for weakness, her own bright, clear-headed, intelligent little self. He was once more making up the fire. Turned round at the sound of her voice, to find her sitting up in bed laughing at him.

"Prince Charlie! I'm ashamed of you! You dir-ty boy! Don't you know what tongs are made for?"

Then she laughed at him again! A faint little laugh though, and so exhausting that after it she fell back on the pillows, scant of breath.

The laugh aroused the mother, trained by love to awaken at the least sound. She sprang to her feet and hastened to the bedside. When she saw the change for the better in her child, the smile on the little face, thankfulness overwhelmed her.

Never had waking moments been more sweet. It was less like waking than like a dream itself. She hugged Gracie to her bosom; just escaped crying over her.

Masters smilingly humoured the child—a little tyranny is a welcome sign in a patient; said, suiting the action to the word:

"Well, I'll use the coal scoop, as you object so to my hands."

"Look at your fingers! Isn't he a dirty boy, mamma? I mustn't let him touch my clean nightgown, must I?"

It was a challenge! Masters saw through the ruse. Her desire was that he should make pretence he wanted to catch hold of her. Then she would struggle to escape him. It was a game she was very fond of—he was to catch her after a long while—and then the romp would begin all over again. Fearing to excite her, he took no notice of the thrown-down glove; merely remarked:

"Well, you look all the better for your sleep." Added, with a smile: "Both of you, I mean."

The mother's heart was too full to speak. Her child was hers once more. Had come back to her from out the Valley of the Shadow of Death. After a long pause she managed to look up at him, tears bedewing her eyes, and inquire:

"And you?"

"Don't worry about me! I am as right as right can be. Just let me go to your bath-room, will you? I shall emerge from it as fresh as the proverbial lark."

"You will stop to breakfast—"

Gracie caught the suggestion in a moment; interposed eagerly:

"Oh, yes, Prince Charlie! You will! Won't you? Have breakfast with me—out of my own tea service."

"Very well. I'll have a bath, and then come and breakfast with you, Gracie—out of your very own cups and saucers and plates. That's understood."

He went to the bath-room. His matutinal cold water sponge was a thing he would have missed dreadfully. During his absence, the doctor paid an early morning visit.

Masters was pleased when he returned to the sick room to see the happy look on the mother's face. Gracie was out of danger the doctor had said. Was going on splendidly—thanks, she said, to——

"To Prince Charlie, mamma! I heard the doctor say so. He's a fairy prince who comes and saves little girls."

Gracie held Prince Charlie with one hand; her mother's with the other, as she spoke:

"Prince Charlie, I want to kiss you."

He submitted to the wish of the little autocrat. Both her arms went round his neck as she gave him what she called her extra nicest.

After that there was a happy breakfast party. The cups were very small; Gracie, propped up with pillows, had to fill them many times. But that was just as well; the greater demand, the greater her pleasure.

The plates, too, were not quite large enough to hold ordinary slices of bread and butter. But then, as Gracie explained, you could hold your bread in your hands, couldn't you?

As for the cups, small cups were very fashionable—mamma had told her so. It wasn't good manners to eat and drink too much; even if you were

- 86 -

ever so hungry. But it was quite good form to say the tea was hot even if it was quite cold. That was part of the game.

The child's daily improvement was of the rapid kind. In less than a week she was skipping about the room. In ten days, well wrapped up, was playing—literally skipping—on the sun-lit sands.

And during the ten days? The author and the mother drifted apart! As the child's convalescence became assured his visits grew less in number; shorter in length.

From visiting three times a day his calls came down to once. His usual hour's visits were curtailed. He stayed but a quarter of that time.

When the child asked a reason, he was busy, he said. But the mother, listening, was not for a moment deceived. Read in his eyes that there had been no removal of his doubt of her. Her pride rose—rose higher and higher and higher day by day.

Her struggle was a hard one, to keep the bitter resentful feeling down. She endeavoured to stifle it with thought of the gratitude she owed him. But it was hard, terribly hard. She was not of a lachrymose temperament at all, but her eyes often tear-filled when she thought of him.

He was cold to her; grew more so; coldly courteous and reserved. Instinctively he feared his own weakness. Kept so close a guard upon himself, so firm a brake upon his feelings, that intercourse with him became depressing and wearying.

There was no longer the old easy flow of talk; words came with difficulty; conversation was an effort on both sides. Forced conversation is usually a failure.

She saw clearly that but for his love for the child—and that, she knew, was genuine—he would not have come to the house at all. She felt that all the while he spoke to her courteously and politely, he was suspicious of her. She showed nothing of her indignation; that would only have been acknowledgment of the hit.

Suspicious of what? She asked herself; asked not once, but a hundred times a day. Her pride would not allow her to put the question to him; so they drifted further and further apart. To her it seemed as with Ichabod: the glory had departed.

Sorry? She was heart-broken over it. She had not learned to love him: she had cared for him all along. More even than she had known, more than she knew even now. The sweet, helpful gentleness of his care for her child when sick, had shown him in a light in which few women would have failed to admire—nay, more than that: to love him.

He was a veritable Prince to her; she could have worshipped him. Her soul had gone out to him—and his to her—so naturally she had scarce noticed its passage. She felt she had known him all her life; so perfectly their thoughts and views seemed to dovetail one another.

There had been no shaping and moulding and rubbing off of corners; no making of rough edges to fit evenly; all that is usually the work of time. It is said that there is no soul but somewhere on this crowded earth another soul responds unto its needs. The meeting is still a rarity, but kindly old Time goes on with his everlasting pruning and polishing and planing down to suit mutual requirements.

He has them—has the man with the scythe and hour glass—in his workshop; hundreds and thousands of young couples. He lets them rub along together, Fate having joined them, until the roughnesses are all worn away and it is scarcely noticeable—certainly not by the young people themselves—that they were not expressly made for each other.

The manufactured article produced in that workshop of Old Time is durable and generally gives satisfaction. Looks so much like the real thing that most people want nothing better. Some people prefer it even, take more pride in it.

Besides, the Merchandise Marks Act is not in force in regard to this particular class of goods, so there is not much loss. It all bears the same label, and there is no penalty for deceiving the public. It is all marked—hall marked: Love.

Sometimes, however, it happens that two souls come together whom Nature has really designed and moulded each to each. It is fraught with much sweetness, such a meeting; sweetness as of music. The harmonies are so perfect and so pure, it seems no power in Heaven or Earth could destroy the enduring melody by a jarring note.

The swelling tones would rise and fall and echo, long after the discordance had subsided. Real love is very rare, rarer than gold and diamonds, but it is found sometimes. In out-of-the-way places, too; wholly unsought, conjoining the hearts of man and woman by the closeness and perfection of their union and coincidence.

She had come to think, and he had thought so, too, that God had framed them so, the one to the other. Fight the idea as she would, in her woman's weakness she thought so still. He, in his manly strength, endeavoured to crush the thought as it rose in his bosom.

But it was there to crush.

CHAPTER XIX

PLAYING THE SPY

When the child had passed all the signposts on the road of convalescence, had reached perfect health, Masters ceased his visits to the bungalow. His interest in Gracie induced him not to avoid meeting her on the front.

The child was all warmth and affection and love for the man she was going to marry. The mother hid her aching heart behind a smile: a woman's usual veil. It was not what a novelist describes as a sad sweet smile; it had degenerated into an hysterical, jerky, clattering, little laugh.

The weather continued fine; the author prolonged his stay. For that reason—anyway, for his own satisfaction he set down that as the cause—he stayed on at Wivernsea.

Not a day passed but he met his little sweetheart. Not a day passed but the breach between the man and woman widened. Soon the conventional greeting at meeting and parting came to be dreaded by each.

They dared not look into each other's eyes. As hands met for those two brief moments, each involuntarily looked away from the other. Fingers were clasped limply; fell away awkwardly. Heartiness, even of the faintest description, was sadly lacking in the shake.

One morning he had a letter from his lawyers. It called for his attendance in London; a question of making an affidavit over some copyright infringement. He resolved to catch the fast train up, and so be able to get back by the fast evening train down.

He was at the station early, having inquiries to make. A parcel of books sent down to him had, by reason of the railway company's vagaries, not reached him. Those inquiries made and satisfied, he purchased newspapers.

Messrs. Smith and Son occupied a space in the booking office. As he dealt with the juvenile representative of the great Strand firm, he was standing with his back to the ticket pigeon-hole. He was presently startled by hearing a voice he recognized, saying:

"First-class, return, London, please."

He turned round sharply, expecting to see the mistress of Ivy Cottage; he could have sworn to her voice anywhere. A woman plainly dressed, almost shabbily, with a long thick veil, stood purchasing the ticket. She repeated the demand; the ticket seller had not caught the words.

Hearing it a second time, Masters had no shadow of doubt about the voice's owner. There were no two voices like it in the world. But the costume amazed him; could only be explained one way.

Not a pleasant way, either. It was a disguise! Masters felt certain of it. She had always been well, expensively dressed. Now, by reason of that, the change was the more striking.

There were three minutes before the train was due; five minutes passed before it arrived. The shabbily-dressed woman paced the platform. Masters watched her from the waiting-room window; five minutes of utter misery.

The station bell rang a second time, the train came in. The veiled woman hurried to a first-class carriage in front of the train. The guard opened a door and she entered one of its compartments. A moment after Masters had entered another.

His purchases at the bookstall lay on the seat beside him all the way to London; he did not read a line of them. For two whole hours he sat stonily looking out of the window, thinking. Thinking, as well as the numb feeling of wretchedness and horror holding him would allow.

It was the first really cold day of the approaching winter. With a view to travelling in comfort, Masters had unpacked, and was wearing a long heavy ulster. It changed his appearance altogether. He knew that, and, bred of the knowledge, there came a desire to track the woman in the other compartment.

With his coat-collar up, she would not be likely to recognize him. It would be possible to follow her and see what this mysterious disguise and flight to London meant; whether she was really as black as his suspicion painted her, as appearances represented her.

Was it a gentlemanly thing to do?... He did not pause to answer his own question. Curiosity and the desire, the necessity, to either set at rest or confirm his fears outweighed everything. Any certainty is better than suspense; we always say so and feel it so—until that certainty is known.

His mind was quickly made up: to follow her. Besides, how could he tell but what she might have need of him; the disguise led to the thought of such a possibility. Masters' was a fertile brain; a dozen such possibilities entered his mind at once. Disguise very frequently meant danger. If that were the case it was his duty, as a man, to shield her.

He would not fail her—so he argued with himself. A desire to do any particular thing causes us to find reasons for its justification; excellent reason. He had made up his mind to follow her.

At Charing Cross the woman in the front part of the train alighted.... Got into a hansom cab.... Masters got into another. A disturbing recollection came to him of a private detective in one of his own books who had acted in similar fashion. But he was not deterred by it.

"Where to, sir?"

Through the trap in the cab roof the inquiry came. Looking up he answered the driver:

"Keep that hansom in sight. I want to see, and not be seen—do you understand?"

"I'm fly."

As the Jehu answered he shut one eye. Then, as he closed the trap, said to himself:

"Man from the Yard—what's she been a-doin' of, I wonder?"

The first cab went over Westminster Bridge, turned into Lambeth, pulled up outside a corner public house. The second cab slowed down and passed the first at walking pace. The woman was paying her fare. Then she entered a door on the glass panels of which were inscribed the words:

BOTTLE AND JUG DEPARTMENT

Masters' cabman knew his business; promptly reined in his horse just round the corner.

"That do you, sir?"

He put the question as Masters alighted, and was feeling in his trousers pocket; the driver continued:

"She's gone into the *Green Dragon* round the corner, she has. We passed the pub a minute agone."

Masters winced. Then reflected that the cabman was only fulfilling his duty zealously. Rewarded him with a half-sovereign.

"Going back, sir?"

Golden fares are rare enough to be worth looking after for a return journey.

"Perhaps—I don't know."

"I'll be stopping here, sir—here, for half-an-hour if you should want me, sir."

Masters nodded.... Passed through a door brass-plated with the words:

HOTEL ENTRANCE.

A flight of stairs faced him. To the left was another door, glass-lettered with the word:

SALLOON.

Into the saloon Masters went. Square panels of bevelled ground glass pivoted on their centres along the top of the bar, shielding the occupants of the saloon from the gaze of those in the opposite bar.

As he entered, Masters heard the woman he had followed enquiring over the bar:

"Mr. Rigby? He is staying here—he expects me."

The hesitation in the enquiring voice made the barman look up. Nervousness in women is rather an uncommon thing to find in the bar of a Surrey-side public-house.

"Oh, yes. But you've come in the wrong way. Round the corner and in at the hotel entrance. You'll find him on the second floor, room 15."

She went out. The bar-tender crossing to him, Masters called for a whisky and soda. Tasted, then tilted the glass, and let the contents be soaked up by the sawdust on the floor. It was not a drink which he thought likely to benefit him. The Lambeth blend of whisky did not somehow seem to tickle his palate.

Watching through the saloon door, he presently saw the veiled woman come in through the hotel entrance, and ascend the stairs. Allowing half-a-minute to elapse, he passed out and followed in her steps. As he commenced the ascent of the second flight he heard a door close; guessed it to be the door of room No. 15.

Reaching the passage on the second floor he noted that the door of room No. 14 was shut. No. 15 was shut too. No. 16 was open. He paused on its threshold. Cast an eye round; not a soul was in the passage; entered. Then the door of No. 16 was shut too; shut, and the key turned on the inside.

A hurried glance satisfied him that it was an unoccupied room. He was glad of that; an explanation that he had entered to wash his hands would suffice, should need of such excuse arise. All the rooms, he guessed, were bedrooms on that floor.

A door was in the dividing wall of Nos. 15 and 16. To that Masters applied his ear. A sense of the contemptibility of the action was strong upon him; yet he could not refrain from acting so.

Something crossed his mind about the end justifying the means. It was a principle he had always violently combated; practice and theory are sometimes at variance. Shame was merged into a feeling of gladness: that there was no key in the lock; it made hearing easier. And he meant to go the whole length; to listen.

As he did so, reflected that such a despicable act as eavesdropping would have been impossible to him a month ago. Suggested to himself that she had brought him to it.

That is men's way—even the best of them.

CHAPTER XX

A HORRIBLE REVELATION

The man she had inquired for in the bar, Rigby—he guessed it was he—was speaking. A husky-toned voice, but the listener could plainly catch the words:

"There! Don't cry, old girl. I have broken my promise to you, I know. You thought I had gone out of England, and I haven't. Well, I am going—going early to-morrow."

"Dick!"

"Gospel truth, old girl. When I said good-bye last time, I meant it. But I got in with the boys and it was the old story. You know; I needn't tell you. I don't blame the boys; they think it a lark, that's all. First one comes and then the other, and each one doesn't know how far I've gone already. I have myself to blame; no one else. I have been lying here over a fortnight with the D.T.'s—came out of them two days ago. Doctor says I shall be able to go abroad to-morrow. He's a good sort; says the Mediterranean cruise will be the thing to set me on my legs. You said so; he says so. He has been kind enough to see to things, booked my berth, and I am going to-morrow from St. Katharine's dock on *La Mascotte*."

"Dick!"

"I am speaking honest, old girl; I am going. I might have gone without writing to you to come up and see me, and you would have been spared this, but I couldn't. I felt that I wanted to say good-bye, old girl, because—because you've been so good to me—more than I deserve. Because," there was a quaver in the speaker's voice, "because I believe it will be the last time."

"Dick!"

The listener, a fierce pain at his heart, heard the catch in her voice, the gasping way in which she ejaculated the name. The man continued:

"It is possible to travel too far on the downward road. So far that you get lost for ever and ever in the valley. I have been down a great big distance. There is a presentiment in possession of me that, somehow, I shall never come back to England. That I shall never come back to worry you again!"

"Dick! Dick! Dick!"

The listening man could hear the heart-breaking sound; the woman's sobs as she spoke. Despite Rigby, despite all, his heart went out to her. Involuntarily he stretched out his arms. They fell to his side again, empty. There was the door between.

"Don't cry. After all, it is perhaps for the best. See what a failure I am. If I drink myself to death perhaps it would be best. Pity it takes so long, that's all. See how like a blackguard I have behaved to you."

The listener could not see, but he knew her actions to be expostulating.

"Ah, it's so; it's so.... I know; I'm sober now. When I come out of it I lie thinking, thinking, thinking. Realize then what a foul beast I have made of myself. When I think how I have behaved to you—to you, my staunch, devoted, dear old pal, the one soul who has stuck to me through thick and thin, I hate myself, I hate myself; and I wonder you don't hate me too."

"You know I love you, Dick. You know that no soul in the whole world loves you as I do."

"Somehow I'd rather see you fly into a rage and call me all the evil names you could invent than look at me so lovingly and sadly; I would indeed. I should feel more that I had deserved to lose you; it would hurt less. But I know you love me; that is one reason why I have determined on trying this Mediterranean trip. Do you know, before I sat down to write to you yesterday, I made a balance of my hands. Held the pen in one and a razor in the other——"

"Dick! Dick! Oh, for God's sake don't talk so!"

"You would never have known, Mab. I am staying here in the name of Rigby. You don't read the police intelligence in the papers. If you had, you would never have linked an account of a drunkard's suicide in a Lambeth hotel with me. You would have thought me on blue water, keeping my promise to you."

The man at the door could hear the sounds of her grief still. It was agony to him; he ground his teeth. That she should suffer so, and he so close, so helpless to help her!

"The pen won the day, Queenie." The speaker was trying to infuse a note of cheeriness. "Don't cry, old girl; there is nothing to cry about after all. I'm here right enough. I wrote you to come up; to say good-bye to the man who has wronged you so. If I live through the trip I shall come back a better, sounder, healthier man. With the courage to fight this drink devil for life or death, for all I am worth."

"And, please God, conquer him, Dick!"

"And what about yourself, little woman? Have you been ill? You look worn out, worn and thinner. You haven't been worrying about me?"

"No, Dick; about Grace. She has been ill; dying once, I thought, but thank God she is as well to-day as ever she was."

"Our little Gracie has been as ill as all that? Poor little soul! And I've been drinking from morning till night, selfish brute that I am, without any thought for you or her. Good God! Why was I born—answer me that?"

The listening man had started back, horrified at the speaker's use of the word, Our. So stupefied was he that he hardly heard the latter part of the man's speech. So, then, this drink-sodden being, posturing under the name of Rigby, was the father of Gracie! Of the little girl he had helped to nurse back to life.

He shook off the numbness which had gripped him; there was more to hear. The thread was taken up again; the mother was speaking:

"——for us to love each other dearly, Dick, all through our lives. Let that be reason enough. Banish those presentiments of yours, dearest. Go bravely on this voyage. It must benefit you, give you strength—moral strength."

"I am a pretty nice sort of beauty to be thinking of moral strength——"

"Don't turn away from me like that; I can't bear it! Pray for strength, Dick; pray for it! Oh, come back to me, Dick dear, your old, old self. My heart aches for you all the while you are away from me. Come back to me, Dick, come back to my loving arms, stronger and better—yourself."

"I'm going to, old girl—going to try hard this time. I can be stronger when I am away from the boys. On board *La Mascotte* there won't be a soul I shall know. It will be torture for me to travel in solitude, for I don't expect such a wreck as I am will make friends. I carry my story written on my face; every man can read it first glance. At the same time, there will be safety in it. From the time I set foot on deck till the time I come back—if ever I come back——"

"Dick!"

"I'll only take claret; will not touch a drop of spirits; so help me God!"

The listener thought he heard a sigh, a despondent sigh, as the man uttered this resolution; probably it had been so resolved before. But it might have been fancy; the dividing door was too thick for him to hear with certainty.

"God will help you, Dick. He must. I believe you, Dick, I believe you. You mean well, and you will succeed. You will come back, and we shall be happy. My dear, dear old Dick; happy again, I know it."

"We will hope so, Queenie."

"Another man, Dick! A strong, healthy and well man. And what I am praying to see, Dick—for I think the tie will help you to keep straight—well and able to marry."

There ensued a moment's silence. The listener's imagination supplied the gap. What he had seen at the back of the bungalow at Wivernsea helped him thereto. He heard the passionate sobbing; the impact of their lips. Then he heard no more.

A great blurring veil seemed to come over sight, hearing, even faculty; to enshroud him. He staggered away as if physically injured. What he had heard hurt so.

On the other side of the door were Gracie's mother, Gracie's father. And they were talking of his coming back from a voyage well enough to marry.

His thoughts went away. Were of that sweet, innocent little child down at Wivernsea. As she came before him he almost groaned; it was too terrible, too horrible. Poor little Gracie!

Trembling fingers unlocked the door; he got downstairs somehow; down to the level of the bar. Called for brandy there, and, regardless of its quality, swallowed it.

It was a mechanical act. Instinct told him that he needed brandy, and he wanted to be doing something; inaction at that moment was maddening.

He walked outside.

CHAPTER XXI

THE ONLY WAY

The cabman was of a speculative nature. Had hung on the chance of Masters' needing to return. Half-sovereign fares are not picked up every hour in the day; the man who dispensed them was worth waiting for.

"Where to, sir?"

The query called down through the trap in the cab roof. The reply was:

"Back again."

Directions so given, because, for the moment, the fare could think of nowhere else.... The cool air blowing on his face gradually brought him back to his usual clear perception of things; he remembered.

The woman he loved so, was lost and dead to him; he quite realized that. Knew too that he loved her still; would do anything to ensure or bring about her happiness. Pity—heart-felt, whole-souled pity—was mingled with his feeling for her now.

Pondering over his position, he came to think of her as more sinned against than sinning. Almost joined in the prayer that the man she loved—whose existence was a bar to his own success—might return well enough to marry.

For Gracie's sake too—sweet, winsome little Gracie! If the man returned well enough to marry it would silence tongues. Surely it was a good prayer.

Then Gracie would grow up knowing nothing of her childhood. No bar sinister would, anyway, be apparent on her escutcheon. She could travel her road in life without a dark shadow o'erhanging it.

If he returned well enough to marry! Why shouldn't he? Or was he, in the solitude which he feared, likely to become despondent again? Was he not more liable to be so, in abstinence from those accustomed stimulants? Despondent even to the clutching of a razor again?

What manner of man was he that had stolen the heart of Gracie's mother? What manner of man was he who could have led astray so pure, so loving a soul?

Surely Rigby had spoken rightly; it were best for such a man no longer to cumber the earth. And yet—that was not the only consideration. There was another. Two: Gracie and her mother.

The man had said that he feared solitude. Had spoken of his personal appearance with loathing. Had feared that no soul would wish to speak to him; that Drink was written on his face. Even allowing for exaggeration, there must be a basis of truth.

Was it wise to let him spend that voyage alone? Was it not possible to send with him a companion? One who would interest him; divert his thoughts; take him out of himself?

A companion to do this for her sake—for her child's sake. Why not himself? What was there in it after all? Not even self-sacrifice. Masters felt that a voyage would do him good. That to stop in England just then, where he was, would stifle him. Let him go on to the broad ocean where he would be able to breathe.

His work he could take with him. Write as well, better, on the ship than in his own rooms. Why not? There was a soul to help to save! There was a woman to be made happy! A child to be taken out of the range of the pointed finger of shame! Why not?

If it were true, as the mother said, that he had saved the child's life, was it to be saved only that she should suffer misery thereafter? Undeserved misery in all the future years? Should he not prevent that if he could?

Himself! Who better fitted? His heart and soul would be in the act. He would be working for those he loved! What a triumph if he could restore this man to her Well Enough To Marry. Why not?

Resolution: he would go. Yes, he would go on to the boat: it was the only way. The cab passed a bill-poster's hoarding. A drama being played in London just then was: *The Only Way*. The mind of the man in the cab had run in keeping with the theatre announcement. He thought of Sidney Carton.

He would go! The hero of that *Tale of Two Cities* was not the only man who had made sacrifices for the woman he loved; although his own sacrifice was hardly worth such a name. In his heart he wished it greater.

The thought trembled through his mind, result of the years of journalistic labour, that his cruise would serve in affording a supply of copy. He hated himself for the thought; it seemed to sully the purity of his motive, his love. He wanted to give to the woman he loved whole-souled service. Yet was weak enough to want an excuse.

 Sidney Carton, when his good work was accomplished, died on the scaffold. When Masters had accomplished his good work—well, there would be time enough to think of that later.

Life was worth living just then: for her sake. It would have little value to him after; after its work was over. Then he would be content, wishful to rest.

The cab had reached Parliament Street. The fare's hand went through the roof trap; the driver reined up.

"There is a passenger—ship's passenger—agent's, somewhere round here," he called up to the bending-down driver, "Cockspur Street, I think; do you know it?"

"So many about, sir. Might you happen to know the name, sir?"

"M'no. Yes! I have just remembered it: Sewell and Crowther."

"Oh, yes; I know the place, sir. Do you want to drive there?"

"Please."

"Right, sir."

A few minutes later the cab stopped and he was alighting at the passenger agents' door. Entering, he said to the counter clerk:

"You are booking for *La Mascotte*, leaving for the Mediterranean, aren't you?"

"Yes, sir; we're the agents."

"Have you any berths left?"

"Oh, yes, sir, a number. It's an off time of the year, and we do not fill up from London. We are stopping at coast stations. We shall fill up from those."

"Let me see a plan of the ship."

"Yes, sir.... That's it. Which class—which part of the boat do you want, sir?"

Masters ignored the question. Pointing to the pen and ink list of names, inquired:

"These are the names of those who have already booked their passages?"

"Yes, sir."

Having located what he wanted he turned to the plan of the ship again, saying:

"This is a two-berthed cabin. One berth is taken, I see. Is the other vacant?"

"Yes, sir. But you can book one in an empty cabin if you like. You will have more room, unless we fill up."

"Thank you. I prefer this one. I think I happen to know the Mr. Rigby who has the other half."

"Oh, I see, sir—friend of yours—of course, companionship. I beg your pardon."

Masters paid his passage money; booked in the name of Charleigh; inquired the time of sailing on the morrow.

"Tide serves at noon, sir. The vessel will go out on top of the water."

"From St. Katharine's?"

"Yes, sir.... Good-day, sir, and thank you.... Not that way, sir.... This door on the left.

"Good-day."

The cabman was waiting. Stooped down from his perch to receive instructions.

"The Telegraph Office, Charing Cross."

There the fare despatched a wire to his Wivernsea landlady; telling her to pack everything of his in his portmanteaux, and send them up by the afternoon train to the care of the Cloak Room, Charing Cross.

Then he drove to his publishers. He would be away some time, and there were certain business arrangements to be made.... Then to his flat in Shaftesbury Avenue. He slept there the night.

More correctly, he spent the night there. Spent it in pacing to and fro, recalling all the events of that long last month. All the happiest days; all the most miserable ones.

He was heart-full of pity for the woman, poor soul! Wished he could wipe away the bitterness of his words that night on the seat at Wivernsea. That was impossible. But he could try to make amends.

In the early morning—dawn just lightening the sky—he wrote a note to Gracie's mother: directed it to Ivy Cottage. Just a purely formal little letter, saying he was called away on urgent business and would not return to Wivernsea again.

As coming from an author it was a disappointing note; there was nothing clever in it. Most authors' notes, perhaps because literary fireworks are supposed to be contained in them, are disappointing.

He sent his fondest love to his little sweetheart Gracie, and expressed a sincere hope for her mother's future happiness. That letter later on in the morning he dropped into a post office.

Gracie's mother, who had journeyed home by the previous evening's train, read it, dry-eyed.

The dryness which burns.

CHAPTER XXII

WHITE LIES

Masters gathered in his luggage from Charing Cross cloak room; reached St. Katharine's Docks with it; got aboard *La Mascotte*.

He was first in the cabin; was arranging his things in an orderly way when Mr. Rigby came aboard. The second tenant of the cabin looked every bit of the wreck he had painted himself.

The author, quick of observation, gauged him to be a man of twenty-five or thereabouts. Younger possibly, but dissipation is an artist who graves deep lines; wrinkles are ageing things. Still of fine physique, but dull-eyed, heavy, face bluish and swollen.

Masters, sweeping a comprehensive glance round, brushed up the new comer with it; said generally:

"I am first to take possession. It seems we are to be close companions on this voyage; too close, in one sense."

He referred to the size of the cabin; then stretching out his hand, continued:

"Let me introduce myself. William Charleigh, journalist. I sincerely hope we shall be very good friends whilst we are together."

The gloom on Dick's face lighted; his colourless horizon seemed brightened; it was as if the sun had suddenly popped out. This cheerful, strong-looking man making overtures of friendship, dissipated all his fearsomeness of solitude on the voyage. Eagerly gripping the hand held out, he shook it long and earnestly; saying:

"I reciprocate that! Thanks! My name's Rigby. Nothing by profession and very little better by nature. I have just come out of—out of an illness. I am taking the trip in the hope of—of getting well."

"No trip like it!" Masters' response was cheerily uttered. "Take my word for that. I took the voyage some years ago, and it pulled me off the grave's brink."

"Really! You look so strong and well I should not have thought you'd had an illness in all the days of your life."

Lies, white lies, came to Masters' lips with the readiness of fiction flowing from his pen; he said:

"I went to the dogs and the dogs nearly did for me. That's an unpleasant way they have when you get inside the kennel. It's a mere shave I'm here talking to you. I pulled up just in time."

"No!"

There were both astonishment and eagerness in Dick's question; both of the most intense kind. Masters' lying was very successful. He was acting so with a view to drawing his companion out.

If a confession could be got from the sick man it would help. Dick would rely for strength and help on the man he had confessed to. That was only human nature.

If you tell a man your troubles he is more than likely to want to tell you his own. A keen observer was Masters; knew that confidence begets confidence. So himself became very confidential.

"It is a fact," he continued. "Like a great number of others, I liked society, and cards, and wine, and—well, I am quite cured now, so I don't mind confessing it. I sacrificed at the shrine of Bacchus too often, and Bacchus resented it. The drink god is an ungrateful sort of deity, isn't he? He sent me visions of snakes and other creepy-crawlies. When I came out of the land of visions I was the most washed-out wreck you ever saw. The doctor gave me up."

"No?"

Dick ejaculated the word almost breathlessly. His own doctor had not gone so far as that. There was more than a chance of hope, after all! He listened.

"Fact. When I heard that, I was on the verge of suicide. Then they put me on a boat doing the Mediterranean trip; just as this one is. This brings back old times, and—well, here I am, you see; I am all right now."

"And the doctor, you say—but how did you—did you conquer your craving?"

"Sheer force of will. I took an oath that whilst I was on the ship I wouldn't touch a drop."

"I have done that, too!"

"You?"

Masters started round in astonishment: really a clever piece of acting.

"Yes.... Well, the cat's out of the bag now. Thank God I haven't got a temperance crank for a companion on the voyage. I have done what you have done, and I am setting out to do now what you did: coming away to get shut of it all. To try and break myself free from the curse."

"You'll do it!"

The flushed face flushed still deeper; deepened to purple, at the assurance. But the dulled eyes had quite an eager light in them, as the speaker pressed his question:

"You think I will? You really think I will? That I have strength enough?"

"Of course! It's the despondent times you have to fear; just don't fear them. Just hang on to me when you feel them coming. Don't get by yourself; it's like taking one's pill uncoated; cling to me like a barnacle. I'll help you to kill your blue devils!"

"You will? By God!" He spoke almost breathlessly; the proffered help was so sweet: hit him in the face. "You're a brick! And a stranger, too; never set eyes on me before!"

"Never. Quite right; never set eyes on you before! But remember, we've been burnt in the same fire. A fellow-feeling makes us—you know the rest."

"By Jove! You are wondrous kind. Do you know, I funked this voyage; funked it believing there was death aboard—overboard—for me. Imagined every soul would read the story in my face and shun me. People are so apt to judge the quality of a pasture by the length of the grass."

"Rot!"

Masters was shuddering inwardly as he looked at his companion. This bloated youth, who looked five-and-twenty, yet spoke with the boyishness of eighteen. He dived into his secret apprehension; shuddered to think that the woman he loved should be linked to such a drink-sodden wretch. Thought of her induced him to lower the sail of his dignity.

There was the hope, the chance, of reformation. When Rigby set foot on the vessel it had been with despair at his heart; he had attended the funeral of hope long ago. Things were different now. As for Masters, he realized that the man was young; might perhaps still meet with salvation.

But it was a thin reed on which to rely: his youth; a two-edged fact: might cut either way. Masters was quite aware of that as he uttered the reassuring monosyllable. Spoke in a forced tone of conviction; there is a limit to suffering; none to fear.

The odds, too, are against a drunkard's reformation; all Lombard Street to a China orange. Anyway, it was a fact he was going to do his level best to turn things to good account. The youngster must be spurred on; not to advance is to retreat. Not only is courage needed in facing a difficulty, but the ability to grapple with it; if looked in the face too long, it is apt to stare us out of countenance.

"I believe you." Rigby spoke with grateful fervour. "Anyway, I am not going to face the future gloomily now!"

"That's half the battle. After all, life's only a journey; it's more or less our own fault if we don't make a pleasure excursion of it."

"I believe that."

"I know it. Remember, I have been in the battle, and came out upper dog. So long as you win the race, what does it matter whether you had a good start or not?"

"Anyway, I shall keep you to your word. If I feel that awful thirst coming on me; feel, as I have felt, that Hell's got its doors gaping wide open for me, I shall worry you."

"You won't; not worry me. Come that moment you hear the hinges start creaking, and we'll try, try together, to keep the doors shut."

"That you should take all this trouble——"

"Trouble be hanged! Don't you know how easy it is to poke another man's fire?"

Masters' eyes looked honestly into Dick's; he was very honest of purpose. Wanted, with all his soul, to keep those doors closed. For the sake of the woman whose trust had been betrayed; for the sake of the little one. He knew how facile is the descent into Hell. Knew, too, that a man ambitious to make a fool of himself never lacks help.

How shines a good deed in this bad world! The goodness of his own was illuminating Masters' eyes at that moment. And he had no fear of the proverb: that if he conferred a favour he might expect ingratitude. Plainly, Rigby was not built on those lines.

Dick was not much of a psychologist or mind reader. Saw only the honest eyes bright with enthusiasm; found them inspiriting; knew nothing of the inner thought prompting this extraordinary kindness.

His was not an inquiring nature; in his happy-go-lucky way he accepted Fate unquestionably. Help had come in his way, and he snapped at it as suddenly as if it were a dish of snapdragon. In response to Masters' words, he mentally thanked his stars, physically held out his hand. In silence, gratefully gripped his companion; was too thankful to speak.

Masters resumed his assumption of cheerfulness. Knew the difficulty he had to face before he spoke: putting seed into the ground does not make a harvest certain; said:

"Now, there is another thing to discuss: about the grub."

"My dear old chap!" Earnestness, conviction in his tone. "I feel as if I shouldn't touch food again for months."

"I know. That's not an unusual symptom." Masters affected to laugh. "I felt like that. And if you go to the saloon table you'll feel like it for quite a while. Look here now!" He spoke suddenly, as if inspired with an idea. "Will you leave your commissariat to me?"

"To you! But why on earth, now, should you be troubled to——"

Masters let a shade of annoyance creep over his face. There was no misreading it. Assuming, too, a tone of regret; he said:

"You mean that? That you would rather I did not interfere?"

The facial expression and voice had the desired effect. Cheated the younger man—surely he must be very young!—into expostulating:

"My dear old chap! For Heaven's sake don't think I mean anything of that sort! I'll do whatever you say."

So he would; that was plainly evident. The strong will had conquered the weaker. Masters felt overjoyed at his success. Most hearts have secret drawers in them containing some good traits: if we can only find the spring.

Moreover, strange as it seemed, Masters was conscious of the birth of a liking for his young companion. He was surprised, too, to realize that he was but a boy. Had thought him five-and-twenty at first; now imagined him to be not much over one-and-twenty years of age—if that.

It was, in a measure, a welcome surprise. His imagination had portrayed Rigby as a hardened debauchee; sunken in vice as sodden in drink. Mingled with the surprise, too, was a feeling of wonder that Gracie's mother should, with one younger than herself——But there, he told himself, there was no accounting for these things; there was no logic or reason in them.

"Very well, then"—Masters speaking, his face cleared of its cloud—"I'll arrange with the steward and the cook. Fresh milk, while it lasts, and beef tea right away till you feel you can compass solidity little and often; that is my prescription."

"You are a good old chap!"

Almost tears in his eyes as he spoke. He had not counted on making friends at all, and here, the moment he set foot on the boat, was one to hand. And such a one! A perfect prince of good fellows.

"For some days," Dick continued, "I shall keep almost to this cabin. Lying down will rest me. Moreover, I am not anxious to show up to the crowd."

Again that purple flush. Masters, considerately, was not looking. Was engaged hanging up his belongings and stowing them away in the limited space at his disposal. It was work which afforded occasion for a considerable display of invention and ingenuity.

The cabin of a three thousand ton vessel, or of an Atlantic liner for that matter, offers little luxury in the way of wardrobe accommodation. Masters, though his personal luggage did not rival in extent that of Beau Brummel, yet found himself in difficulties. He turned to his companion; said:

"I shall be inside a lot too. As a matter of fact, I'm finishing a book; have a lot of writing to do. So you won't be altogether alone."

"That's jolly!"

"Lend a hand here, old fellow, will you? See if we can shove this portmanteau under."

Dick was only too glad to be of service; willingly rendered aid in the stowing away of things. Later followed suit with his own stuff. Masters was intent on keeping his companion occupied even with the smallest matters.

That was the beginning of things. The author felt that he had got the bit in his companion's mouth; that it rested with him which road was taken; depended on his skill as a rider. Still there was every care and caution to be exercised.

When you ride a young colt it is well to see that your saddle is well girt.

CHAPTER XXIII

LOVE'S LABOUR LOST

Prosperity attended the voyage; if that term may be applied to recovery of health. The sea-air—genial companionship had something to do with it—was pulling Dick round. He said he was a new man; received assurance of that fact from inspection of his reflection in the mirror.

Although his story was no longer visible on his face, it was in his heart; hidden away perhaps, but there still. He had left the stepping-stones of milk and beef-tea a long way behind; was walking through square meals as vigorously as any man aboard.

The friendship opened up in the little two-berth cabin had developed into the closest kind. On one side it had started garbed in the mantle of pretence. That was soon shed; sincerity taking its place.

Dick's fidelity was dog-like; he followed his companion about as if loath to lose sight of him. Masters had discovered in him artistic tendencies; the ability to draw well. It was long before Dick's hand ceased to remind one of a jelly; when it did, Masters asked, would Dick oblige him by doing something?

Oblige him? Dick repeated the question. Great Scott! Was there anything he could ask which he, Dick, wouldn't jolly well jump at the chance of doing. What did Charleigh take him for?

The story Masters was engaged on was to be illustrated; sketches were needed of the proposed drawings. So the author said, speaking quite casually.

As a matter of fact, he was anxious to find occupation for idle hands. Feared the provision, if he did not himself provide it, of less profitable work. Remembered a proverb to that effect: Satan filling a stellar part in it.

"Let me make them for you, will you?" Dick spoke eagerly. "I can draw properly, really; I've had drawings in the *Strand* and *Windsor*, and they're particular, you know. I did it because I loved the work; I had to give it up, because my hand——"

Masters interrupted him; was ever anxious to prevent a harking back to the old days of failure. Wanted his protégé to look forward, not backward: at the brightness ahead, not on the horror which he hoped was for ever left behind.

"My dear Dick, a thousand thanks! I shall be only too glad if you will."

That was the commencement of an even closer intercourse; the drawings drew them together. The sketches had to be thought out and considered. On smooth days were worked at with pencil on paper.

Dick's was really a skilled hand. And that hand of his—he took immense pride in the fact—was steady now. The ability is not given to every artist to do line work on a boat. The throbbing from the engine room usually permeates every part of the vessel.

So the two men would sit on deck, one writing and the other drawing. Sometimes the author's pen would suddenly cease work; cease for quite a while. Dick respected those pauses; imagined Charleigh to be thinking out the details of his work.

He was wrong. Masters was thinking of Miss Mivvins. Remorseful thoughts; remorse that he had ever wounded that generous, sweet soul; ever added by his harsh words to her burden of sorrow. Vainly regretful thoughts: regret that he had not met her earlier in life. A sigh usually marked Masters' emergence from dreamland. If he did not directly pick up his work again, his companion would open up conversation; one day said:

"I call you Prince, old fellow, because you told me to. Is it a nickname or your real name?"

Masters smiled; the sweet innocence of his godmother occurred to him; he said:

"Which do you think, now?"

"Well, I can't help thinking that Prince Charleigh seems too happy a combination to be the real thing. Real godmothers and godfathers don't hit on those things usually."

"Mine did not. Yet all the same I was christened, quite recently, Prince."

"Ah!" Dick's eyes sparkled; he fancied himself a discoverer. "I'll bet you a new hat I can guess the sex of the christener—a girl?"

"Splendid marksman! A bull's eye! Hit the centre of the target first time!"

A merry twinkle found place in the younger man's eyes as he inquired:

"Engaged to her, old fellow?"

"Well——"

Masters paused. Then, with a quiet smile and a long puff at his pipe, completed his sentence:

"We have spoken of marriage."

"Soon?"

"M'no. She's very young."

The quiet smile broadened on Masters' face; he remembered how very young!

"I have been writing this morning to my girl," said Dick. "We shall touch port today for stores, and be able to post letters, the Captain says."

"So I gathered."

"Did your ears burn this morning, old chap? My letter was full of you."

"Was it?"

Masters started; was troubled. His pipe was being smoked more vigorously than ever; he continued:

"I am sorry for that."

"Why? I told my girl who was responsible for my salvation. You.... Ah, don't shake your head, Prince. My living, my being here on this deck alive, sane, and, thank God! with a feeling of manhood strong in me, is due to you. But for you, I should have gone overboard.... Yes, I know it; I want you to know that I know it. I can never repay you, that's out of the region of possibility, but you might like to feel that you took a fellow-creature out of the slough, even if the fellow isn't worth much. You saved my life and you've made it worth living—to me, at any rate."

He spoke with a catch in his voice; gratitude moved him. So earnest was his speech of thankfulness that it moved Masters also; Dick went on:

"I came aboard with the knowledge in my heart that I should make a hole in the water. I got my girl up to London, the only friend that has stuck to me, to say good-bye to her. And I meant it, Prince; meant it for a final good-bye, a good-bye for ever. Thanks to you, old chap, that's a thing of the past; the shadow has passed away."

"I hope, Dick—nay, more than hope—I am confident, never to return."

"I pray God so, Prince! I do! I do! I say that reverently. I pray God so. I'm a bit fearful of when this trip is over; just a bit; that's all that's wrong with me. You've been my anchor; I don't know how I shall ride on a tempting sea without you. You are not as other men—no, let me say it—I have clung to you, Prince, old fellow, like—well, like the ivy clings to the oak. I can't help thinking, when the oak's gone what's to become of the ivy."

"You'll go back home well, and find other ties."

Then he gave utterance to the phrase which had been persistently ringing in his ears so long:

"You will go back well enough to marry."

Dick started; smiled. The memory of that last interview came back to him too; he answered:

"That's what my girl says, Prince. But I don't feel at all like marrying: I'm not that sort."

"Not—that—sort!"

It seemed to Masters as if all the blood in his body suddenly turning scalding hot and black-coloured; filled his veins to bursting point. He sat quite still, motionless; fearful that if he moved, loosened for one instant his hold on himself, his feelings would be too much for him.

His trip, his care for Dick then, was so much labour thrown away.... He must keep that feeling, that desire to rush at the boy's throat and choke his worthless life out, keep it down. Nothing would be gained by loss of temper. It is the cool hammer which fashions the red-hot iron; he knew that, yet did not dare to look at his companion.

His stylographic pen was not of the best make; perhaps resented being held down so. The ink ran from it and made a blot on the paper. Although conscious of its existence he allowed the size of the blot to increase; still he made no movement.... At last he spoke; spoke so huskily that Dick looked up from his sketch. The moment he did so, he cried:

"Prince! Good God, old chap, what's the matter? Prince! Prince! You are ill!"

"I am quite well. Sit down; I am all right I tell you. I want to talk to you."

"Rot!"

The boy scrambled to his feet impatiently, looking in amazement at the white, drawn expression on his companion's face; continued:

"You're ill. Think I am blind? Come to the cabin and lie down."

"Sit down."

"Not for half a second!"

As he answered he was cramming the drawing materials into his pocket; continued:

"If you want to talk come into the cabin and lie down. I'll talk to you there till the doctor comes."

"Doctor! Don't be absurd! I am all right. I want to talk to——"

"Then come right along into the cabin out of this sun; talk there. It's my turn to give orders. I'm going."

He moved away as he spoke, throwing a glance over his shoulders: an anxious look. He was fearing greatly for the man whom he had grown to love.

Masters rose; staggered up really. That hot black blood seemed to rise with him, right up to his brain. Had the effect of making things go whirling round and round for a minute. Then with an immense effort he pulled himself together. Better perhaps in the cabin, out of earshot.

He must have his talk out with Master Dick.

CHAPTER XXIV

RESTORED SIGHT

Dick led the way; Masters followed; the cabin was reached. The moment they had entered, the author put his back against the door; spoke with a gravity which alarmed his companion:

"You and I have got to have a talk. Plain talk."

Dick's anxiety was evidenced in the tone of his voice as he said:

"All right, old son. Cackle for hours if you like. But I wish to goodness you'd lie down and see the doctor first."

Masters disregarded this; considered it a flippant, out-of-place remark; in inconceivably bad taste. Moreover, he was disgusted by Dick's evasion; by reason of it went himself the straighter to the point:

"We left off on deck at where you were talking of your girl. You said you were—were not of the marrying kind!"

"Eh? Yes, of course I said so. It is so. But what on earth does it matter what I said?"

Dick still looked anxious. Was making all due allowance for the fact that literary fellows are inclined to be cranks. Yet was doubtful whether the man with his back to the door was not overstepping the limits of legitimate and traditional crankiness.

"It matters a deal!"

Masters uttered these words so fiercely that—in no way relieved—Dick said:

"Does it? Well then, Prince, old fellow, if you're so anxious about my future as all that, I'll relieve your anxiety. I can truthfully tell you that I have never set eyes on a girl yet that I should be at all likely to marry. Wine's been my trouble, not women."

Once more the black blood surged up; a curtain seemed to come up before Masters' eyes; a thick misty curtain blotting things out. But he knew he must keep his temper in hand; exhibit only calmness. He would gain more that way: for the child's sake—for her sake.

"Dick." He spoke with all the earnestness in him. "Awhile back you spoke of being grateful to me. Said you would do anything to—to please me."

"So I would, old fellow; so I would. On my soul I would! But I wish to goodness you would lie——"

Dick's hand was placed soothingly on his companion's shoulder, as he spoke. Masters bore it, but interrupted expression of the wish that he would lie down; said:

"Suppose I put you to the test? If I ask you to marry your girl, will you do it?"

"No!"

Dick answered with a laugh. Despite the anxiety of which he was so full, he could not resist a feeling of amusement at the request; added emphatically:

"I most certainly will not."

Up surged the blood again; anger came into the eyes which flashed so; almost blinded their owner. A step forward, and he seized Dick by the shoulders; held him so firmly, as in a vice.

"Tell me." He was speaking from a throat the dryness of which made it hoarse. "After the way in which you have behaved to her—tell me why you refuse to marry her?"

Dick looked at his companion doubtfully; had not a trace of anger in doing so. Felt that in dealing with him the truth was the only thing; said:

"Refuse to marry her? Why, you confounded old idiot, you! How on earth can a fellow marry his own sister?"

"SISTER!"

Just the one word—he almost screamed it—that was all Masters could utter. He started away and released his hold. Fell back against the door, in the intensity of his astonishment, clutching wildly, unfeelingly, at the panels for support.

Dick's anxiety rapidly gained strength; he became more alarmed than ever. Formed the idea now that this was no passing faintness, but that Masters was seriously ill. Was even afraid to leave him standing there against the door, for fear he should fall. Suddenly, flinging off his coat, he cried:

"You're stronger than I am, and I guess I'll get the worst of it, but here goes."

He stood threateningly in front of the much bigger man, the light of determination in his eyes; continued:

"Will you lie down on that bunk and let me fetch you the doctor? Refuse, and as sure as I stand here I shall try my hardest to make you."

Masters pressed his hands to his aching, throbbing forehead. His mind was whirling so, that it was no wonder he staggered. His brain did not seem able to hold the blend: could not contain so much happiness and so much condemnation of himself, for his unutterable foolishness. True to his threat, Dick advanced; Masters warded him off.

"Don't, Dick! Just a moment, old fellow.... I don't want a doctor. What you have just said has done me more good than a syndicate of all the doctors in the world could effect."

He laughed weakly, foolishly: by no means a confidence-inspiring laugh. The mirth, if such it could be called, and the change of tone were even more disturbing to the listener.

"What have I said? Here, Prince, you are going off your nut, old man; that's what's the matter with you! I thought it when you began this game, but I didn't like to say so; I must now. Sitting in the sun so much has given you a mild attack of sunstroke. If you've any feeling that you would like to knock me about, now's your time to indulge it; for I am going to try to make you come away from that door."

"Dick! My dear boy! I assure you I am all right! All I want is a talk———"

"Talk! Great Scott! Have you done anything else? This has been like a tabbies' tea-fight! There's been enough chatter to keep a tree-full of monkeys going! Talk! Christopher Columbus! It's been a perfect Niagara of jaw!"

"There, I'll lie in my bunk if it will please you, Dick."

"It's that, or sudden death from a blow of this ought-to-be brawny arm! Money or your life was never uttered more seriously than I am talking. The doctor———"

"Don't go for the doctor, Dick, please. I don't need him. I am all right now."

"I've only your word for that; I may tell you that your face doesn't lend any confirmation! You look as if you'd lost your seven senses and couldn't say Bo! to a goose! Are you better?... Really? Honour bright?"

"Yes, yes, yes. Tell me, Dick, if she is your sister, who is Gracie?"

It looked like a turning of the tables! Was Dick's turn to start and exhibit surprise. His was the wide-open-eyed-and-mouthed type of astonishment; showed plainly in his face; deception was a thing unknown to him. A moment's wondering silence; then he inquired:

"Who's Gracie? How the dickens did you know there was any Gracie? Why, she's her kid, of course; my little niece!"

At that the man in the bunk laughed. Almost his old hearty ringing laugh again. But even yet it retained a tone of wildness; he cried:

"Blind! Blind! Blind! What a crass idiot; what a senseless fool I have been!"

Dick scratched his head; these sudden changes of mood were too much for him; said:

"Well, you certainly *are* behaving in first-prize-gold-medal idiotic fashion! But the puzzle to me is, how the deuce did you know anything about little Gracie?"

"Know about her? I actually know her! Good heavens! How clear it all seems now."

"Does it? That's all right! I may be permitted to remark that our ideas on opaqueness would be likely to differ!"

"It was she—oh, Dick, Dick, Dick! Don't you understand?"

"How can I help doing so—when you are so lucid! You brainless old firework, you; let off some more crackers."

"Dick! Dick! It was she, she who christened me Prince!"

"What! Why, you said it was the girl to whom you had spoken about marriage!"

"Quite right."

The idea returned to Dick that there must be something wrong, very wrong—as he put it—in Masters' upper storey. Marriage! With Gracie! It was simply too absurd for words; he said:

"You jibbering old idiot, you, what do you mean? Gracie isn't five years old!"

"I know! I know! I know! And yet a month ago at Wivernsea I promised her, if when she grew up she wanted to marry me—which she won't—that I would."

"Wivernsea! Why, you know my sister!"

Masters started up. Gripped the boy by both shoulders and shook him. Happiness struggled with the tears in his eyes as he said:

"Dick, just a wee while ago—forgive me for it, laddie—I hated you! Now I love you! I love you! I love you! You've told me just the best news I've heard for years."

"That's all right, old man."

He shook himself free, and ruefully rubbing his shoulders, continued:

"What that news may be I don't know; it's beyond my intellect's horizon. However, as it pleases you it's sufficient—so long as it doesn't hurt me. Don't make me black and blue in the exuberance of your affection. As the poet hath it: It's all very well to dissemble your love, but why do you kick me downstairs?"

"I'm sorry, Dick—really sorry. Did I hurt you? I'm so full of happiness that I could kick myself for having been such a fool all this horrible long time."

"You speak in the past tense. Seems to me the foolishness is only just coming to a head!"

"Stop your chaff, there's a good fellow. You can use that later on. Just now it's almost life and death with me. What's your sister's full name, Dick?"

"Full name? Mabel Seton-Carr, of course!"

"Of course! Of course! Of course! Didn't Gracie write it in full in my book?"

"I'll be hanged if I know! I shouldn't think it would add to the book's sale if she did—with my remembrance of her pothooks and hangers. You don't live at Wivernsea, do you? I never heard that there was a lunatic asylum there!"

"Lived there for years!"

"Oh! Then perhaps you knew Mabel's husband, Seton-Carr, when he was alive?"

"When—he—was—alive?"

"Yes. Of course! You blithering old idiot, you; what are you looking at me like that for? You don't think that I am such an utter egregious ass as to suggest that you have known him since his death, do you?"

"How long, Dick—how long—how long has he been dead?"

"Nine—ten months now. Between ourselves, there was not much to regret when he added his signature to the big death-roll. Though it's not customary to speak truth of a man who can't speak for himself, is it?"

"Blind! Blind! Blind! She's a widow! Of course! What a fool—what a fool I have been!"

"Hear, hear—large-sized kind!"

CHAPTER XXV

EJECTED FROM THE CABIN

Masters remained buried in thought for a few moments. The sudden opening of his eyes and the refreshing news were almost overpowering him.

Presently he looked up at his companion, who was watching him closely; said:

"You can't think, Dick, my dear boy, what a big fool I have been making of myself."

"No—I can't. If it was any foolishness bigger than your present size, it must have been simply colossal!"

"You told your sister of me in your letter. Did you mention me as Prince Charlie?"

"Of course!"

"She'll know! She'll guess! I am glad. Thanks! Thanks! Thanks!"

He seized and wrung the hand of the amazed Dick, utterly ignoring his feelings. Only felt that he must do something to relieve his own. He retained just sufficient self-control to keep himself from indulging in a wild dance of jubilation.

Dick, affecting to nurse crushed fingers, made an effort to get to the bottom of things. Usually he accepted circumstances without inquiry as to their source; but suspicion was roused in him now. It was suspicion of a kind that he wanted to make into certainty; he said:

"A few minutes ago you expressed regret that I had mentioned you at all in the letter."

"I know! But a few minutes ago things were all gloomy and black and ugly! Now they are all bright, rose-coloured and lovely. The sun has risen! The pulse of day is beginning to beat!"

"I say, old chap—how much a thousand words do you get for that kind of thing? You roll it off as naturally as water rolls off a duck's back."

"When do we reach London, Dick?"

"Reach London? Are you mad? Why, we haven't turned round on our homeward journey yet!"

"There's some sort of overland route, isn't there? We can get back quicker?"

"Quicker? You are mad! It was only this very morning that you were expressing regret that the time of the trip wasn't going to be double the length!"

"This morning was then! Now is now! Oh, Dick, you stony-hearted, wicked villain you!" He sprang laughingly over to the boy as he spoke. "Why didn't you say before——"

"Keep off!"

Dick, dodging, picked up the first thing his hands rested on and assumed a burlesque attitude of threat as he continued:

"Assault me again with one of your hundred-ton affectionate squeezes, and I'll blow your brains out with this telescope. Throw up your hands!"

"I surrender!"

Masters laughingly fell in with the other's burlesque melodramatic humour; continued:

"I am a bear, but a tamed one. I haven't a squeeze left in me!"

"Perhaps your Royal Highness is saving them up," suggested Dick, his eyes twinkling as he spoke. "I begin to have a grave suspicion—garnered from some of your rambling ravings—that you have designs on my sister!"

"I have, Dick, I have!"

"Open confession is good for the soul! But you don't fool me. I should be false to every sense of brotherly duty if I failed to warn her against your embraces. I shall bear the marks of one of them—on my shoulder—to the grave."

"Dear old Dick!" Masters started forward impulsively: "I am ever so sorry that——"

"Keep off! Keep off! If you don't I'll scream for help!"

Masters' thoughts went off at a tangent. Love is a leveller. Even authors, under the influence of that other circumstance to which all flesh is heir, are not superior to a passion for the conjunction of octavo sheets and pens. It found expression in Masters' exclamation:

"The letters!"

Dick, inexperienced in such matters, failed to understand. His denseness was irritating. He was aware of that, but only with intent to provoke, ejaculated:

"Eh?"

"The letters! Don't you understand? We haven't touched port yet—not near it."

"Four hours off yet."

"Then I shall have time to write to your sister myself."

"What—in four hours? Bold adventurer! If at first you don't succeed, try, try, try, again. Your bravery unmans me! Excuse these tears!"

"Clear out of this cabin, Dick, and leave me to myself. I want to write."

"What! For four hours? I'll be hanged if you do! Four hours of letter from a man in your condition would prove deadly to the woman receiving it. I won't be party to such inhumanity."

"Will you go out?"

"No, I won't! I paid the ship people for half this cabin, and I'm going to assert my rights.... Keep off, Prince Charlie. If you put a finger on me I'll have you tried by court-martial, and sentenced to walk the plank!"

"Will you leave peaceably then?"

"No, I won't; keep off!"

Dick was thoroughly enjoying the situation now; his face was one huge beaming grin as he continued:

"Besides, I am going to write a letter myself. To my sister, warning her against the introduction of a lunatic into the family. She has been good to me, and I shall take this opportunity of making some return for it."

"You wrote your letter to her this morning on deck with the stub of a pencil. Go and write the other the same way."

"Shan't! Can't: want ink. Couldn't describe your vile character in pencil; such labour necessitates ink: black ink."

"Out you go!"

"Keep off!... If you evict me from my cabin—I believe you are a woild Oirish landlord in disguise, you spalpeen—I'll sue you for damages, and have you hanged at the yard arm."

"Out you go!"

That time the boy's dodging ended in failure; his laughter rather handicapped him. The other, laughing triumphantly, caught, struggled with and pushed him out of the cabin. Clapping the door to, bolted it.

Then Masters sought again his berth, intending to indulge in a little castle-building: aerial kind. Dick's tattooing on the door-panels with his fists eliciting no reply, he bent and shouted through the keyhole:

"You bushranging brigand! You buccaneering bandit! You blood-thirsty old skull-and-cross-bones, you! I've just remembered that this is piracy! Piracy on the high seas! I'm going straight to the Captain to get the handcuffs polished up. I'll make it my business to see you go back to England in irons. Put that in your pipe and smoke it."

With that he retired—to the accompaniment of a shrilly whistled Rule Britannia and a tramp as of soldiers. Masters was left the opportunity of writing his love-letter.

He came out of the land of dreams. Sat down at the table, and drew paper and pen towards him, implements of his trade. Spent time in looking at the paper, pen in hand, but no words were formed.

It seemed strange that a man who for many years had gained a living by dexterous juggling with words should be unable to shape them now. But they would not come, to his satisfaction.

"What can I say on paper," he thought, "which will exhibit my awakened conscience? Will be sufficiently contrite and penitent to appeal to her? Nothing! Half the meaning of a letter lies in the reading of it. She would be justified, fully justified, from her present point of view, if she were to throw it into the fire without reading it at all."

A look of gloom settled on his countenance; he asked himself:

"What right have I to write to her at all?—after the way in which I insulted her? To apologise on paper is the act of a coward. I must go to her, and hear her contempt of me. I deserve it."

He did not write his letter after all.

CHAPTER XXVI

AS SOBER AS A JUDGE

That determination of his, to wait, was a hard thing for Masters to adhere to. He knew it was a wholesome resolve; at the same time the pill was very bitter: uncoated kind.

It is so much easier to do things on the spur of the moment; courage is an unbidden lieutenant then. Later on the aid must consciously be gathered together.

Curiously enough, Masters experienced pleasure in making the way hard for himself; there was no attempt to boil the peas before putting them in his shoe. It seemed more just to her whom he had wronged, this penance: a flagellation of his soul, as it were.

"She must witness my utter, abject humility," he reflected. "Must hear my prayer for forgiveness of my doubt of her. My sorrow must be seen; I can't paint it in pen and ink. Whatever I wrote—oh, the voice is mightier than the pen!—she might refuse to forgive me. Besides, if she is forewarned, knows I intend seeking her, she may even refuse to see me. I won't give her the chance; I won't write at all."

That was his decision; the result of half-an-hour's close thought and the consumption of three pipes of tobacco. Then he sought his companion on deck. Braced himself up for the interview, rightly guessing the manner in which he would be assailed.

"Hullo!" Dick grinned. "What have you come up on deck for—inspiration? Think to infuse a sea-kissed salty air in your correspondence? I wouldn't lose any of that four hours if I were you. How many quires of my superfine cream-laid vellum note paper have you consumed so far? I know you haven't got any of your own."

"Not a sheet."

"Eh?"

"I have changed my mind."

"I deny the possibility of that! You haven't a mind to change!"

"I am not going to write a letter at all."

"What! After all this fuss too! Well, I am—there! After those absolutely brutal and unprovoked assaults on me too! Truly has the mountain laboured!"

"What I have to say shall be uttered orally."

"I doubt that! If my sister takes the advice I have given her in this letter, you'll never have a chance of getting within earshot. I have told her that you are the most violent, headstrong, ferocious, wrathful savage I ever met; that you are coming home. I have advised her to flee from the wrath to come."

"You are incorrigible, Dick."

"I like that! For pure and adulterated cheek, that annexes Huntley & Palmers' entire factory! I am viciously assaulted by a rabid lunatic. I am deprived of the use of ink and paper purchased with my own hard coin. I am thrown out of my cabin. And the man guilty of these foul crimes coolly stands in front of me with a pipe and a jeering remark in his mouth. Incorrigible!"

"My dear old Dick——"

Masters commenced a speech so; putting his hand on the boy's shoulder affectionately. He was interrupted by the cry of:

"Hands off!"

Dick assumed an appearance of abject fear, shivering like a calves-foot jelly. It was belied by the grin he could not keep off his face as he continued:

"No more of your affection! I want to walk ashore. I don't want to be carried on a stretcher, maimed for life."

Masters was in earnest: deadly earnest. He wished he could get his companion to veer round from his frivolous mood. There was a slight frown on his face, as he said:

"Will you be serious, Dick?"

The boy was not insensible to the intonation of the words. Looked up, saying:

"Well, what is it?"

"I want to talk to you about your sister."

The opportunity was too good to be missed; appealed irresistibly to the humorous side of the listener; frivolity gained the day. Dick's nature was such that happiness ever wanted to bubble up, and it was so long since he had felt inclined to give it a show. He emitted a groan; leaned back in the deck chair and thrust his hands into his pockets.

"I thought that," he said. "I guessed it! Existence aboard this lugger's going to be made a curse to me! I am going to have her drummed into my ears all the rest of the voyage."

"Dick!"

"Understand, Prince Charleigh, that I know her. Have known her for nearly one-and-twenty years. By your own showing, you have known her little more than a month. ... Very well, two months then. It's out of your power to present her in any light in which I haven't seen her. I know the colour of her eyes, hair and teeth; the tilt of her nose and the length of it; how she looks when she's doing this, and how she looks when she's doing that. You understand? I'm not going to be bored all day long with your two-months old description of her."

"My dear Dick!"

Masters could not help laughing. Concluded that it would be best to let the boy run on. Necessarily he must reach the end of his tether, and his own turn would come then, when, in the natural course of things, the other's exuberance had subsided.

"You may laugh! You're infected. The disease is coursing through your veins. But you're not going to make a victim of me. When you feel it coming on, you just go to the bows—there's never any one there—and rhapsodize to the ship's figurehead. Spare me."

"Dick!"

Masters spoke quite patiently, smiling the while. He was giving the other his head; it was his best, his only, plan.

"Grin on, you old lunatic! But I warn you, if you seek to make my life a misery by pouring lover-like descriptions of my sister into my unwilling ear, I'll abandon myself to the mercy of the ocean, and sneak off alone in the Captain's gig."

"Well, I do want to talk to you about your sister."

Dick groaned again. He was in great good humour; his feet were beating a lively tattoo; Masters continued:

"But I don't propose now, or hereafter, to say one word about her appearance, manner or ways."

"Thanks, thanks, kind sir. For this relief much thanks. Excuse this emotion; they are tears of relief."

There was a limit; Masters was reaching it. Was forced into saying, half seriously, half jokingly:

"You are the most unsympathetic, hard-hearted brute that ever existed."

Dick grinned. It was exactly what he wanted to hear; took the utterance as the greatest possible compliment. He was succeeding admirably; restraining his delight, he said:

"Your flattery is too subtle. You wrap it up too much: like an American caramel. Please remember that my perception is not as delicate as yours."

"There is one thing I wanted to ask you, but whilst you are in this mood, I won't."

 He turned to walk away. Dick realized the possibility of carrying a joke too far; in a minute was all repentance. He would not have wounded his friend's feelings for worlds; called out:

"Come back.... Orate. I'll be as sober as a judge."

He fully meant that.

CHAPTER XXVII

THE FINANCIAL LOADSTONE

Masters walked back to where Dick was sitting; stood facing the boy again. It was plain that he was really worried; evidently had something on his mind. Dick paid as much quiet attention as it was possible for him to bestow as the author spoke:

"You will oblige me very much by listening. This business reminds me of the boys and the frog, and I am not finding the rôle of frog a pleasant one to fill. If you will drop stone throwing and let me croak, I shall take it as a particular favour."

"Croak on."

"When I told you that I had lived at Wivernsea for years, I should have said only a month in each year. I go down there each October."

"This is of absorbing interest!"

Dick's intentions were good, but his high spirits got the better of him. The look on his companion's face induced him to settle for another effort of solemnity.

"It was necessary for me to tell you that; by way of explanation of how little I know of Ivy Cottage!"

"Croak on."

Masters was leaning against the handrail, his fingers handling the ropes which supported the lifeboat. He put both arms through and, resting so, spoke on:

"People in Wivernsea—who don't know your sister—don't speak well of the place, Dick."

"What do you mean—haunted?"

"No. Worse than that."

The gravity in the speaker's manner was not without its effect on the boy. A spasm of pain shot across his face; he sat up soberly enough now. The feet ceased their drumming; the hands came out of his pockets; the air of nonchalance fell from him like a mask.

"Worse? What?"

"That is what I am anxious to have explained. In a sense, it is no business of mine, but I want it cleared up for your sister's sake; and I think you ought to know."

"What?"

"This tittle-tattle I am referring to. It goes to the length of saying that people living at Ivy Cottage go under false names. That not long since, the sheriff was in possession under a warrant of execution and the furniture was seized. Of course, I know they are all lies———"

"You're wrong, Prince. There is a basis of truth in it."

Masters started in surprise. Dick's head was bent, to hide the flush of shame on his face. He spoke in a troubled voice; then suddenly lifted his head; meant to speak honestly, said:

"I am the foundation of that; the miserable cause of that rumour."

"You!"

"Yes. You can't help despising my meanness when I have told you, even if you don't already. It is due to you that I should explain how it came about. I have had drinking bouts similar to the last one you helped me out of———"

"*The* last one."

"Please God—yes; the last one. At the commencement of one of them, about six months ago, I fell an easy victim to some card-sharpers; I was a stranger within their gates and they took me in—literally. I had no more idea what I was playing than I had of the character of the players. A thousand pounds was the amount they said I had lost, and I was too far gone to deny it. Of course I had not that money on me. I was made to sign a cheque they drew on my bankers on a half-sheet of note paper with a penny stamp stuck on it."

"I see."

"I was reaching the shaky stage then, Prince, when the hands need a ton-weight pressure to prevent their acting like aspen leaves. The bank refused payment on the ground of 'difference of signature.' The card-sharping people consulted the six-and-eightpenny fraternity and issued a writ for that thousand pounds. Served it on me whilst I was lying in bed in a state of mental insensibility."

"Is it possible? I wonder the process-server was allowed to enter your room."

"He was the kind that could not be kept out. They had a wily little lawyer acting for them—I found this all out afterwards, of course. He found out the name of the medical man attending me and presented himself as the doctor's assistant; so served me."

"What a beastly trick!"

"Success attended its performance, though. The game was in their own hands, and they were playing it by the end-justifying-the-means rule. Eight days after service judgment was signed and an execution was put in at my sister's house at Wivernsea."

"Why on earth there?"

"Part of the game they were playing. They had made inquiries, and found that I was living in London at the time in a furnished flat. I suppose they relied on my sister paying the execution out."

"Which she did?"

"She flew up to London, and consulted our family lawyer. He looked into the thing at the Law Courts; read the affidavit of service and things of that sort; saw that the whole matter was in order. They came on to see me, but I was in the snakes-on-the-wall stage at the time; didn't know them from Adam and Eve. The family lawyer—one of the best, but rather inclined to look on the breath of scandal as a fatal thing—advised a settlement. Said that, even if she turned the execution out, they might proceed against me in bankruptcy. Pointed out that expenses were piling up, and—well, Sis paid the sheriff."

"How ghastly!"

"I used a stronger word. My adjectives were like fireworks, then I came round and learnt what had been done: but it was too late. All I could do was to give Sis a cheque for what was paid, and ask her to forgive me; which, dearest of dear souls, she has done a dozen times in my miserable life."

Dick looked the picture of dejection by the time he had finished. Masters was not, however, observing him: was following out his own train of thought.

"Of course. That explains. News of a thing like that, and in another name too, would speedily spread over a small place like Wivernsea."

"As easily as jam is spread on a piece of bread. I never thought of that, though. What a beast—what a perfect beast I have been!"

Dick was of an excitable temperament: the alcohol in his thermometer—his spirits—was ever at the fever-heat of exuberance or deep down at the zero of dejection. But little was needed to carry him to either extreme: therein lay his danger. Masters knew it; yet he said:

"If I had only known all this a few weeks ago, I should not be on this boat now."

"I am glad you lacked the knowledge, then, Prince. For if you hadn't come aboard when you did, I shouldn't be here either."

Masters regretted his reproachful speech the moment it was uttered. Instantly changed its tone; put up a warning finger as he cried threateningly:

"Dick!"

"I know it, dear old chap; I know what my intent was. But don't let's talk about it now."

"Or ever again."

The cloud cleared from the lad's face; he responded heartily:

"Right!"

At the moment the gong sounded in the engine-room. An air of bustle pervaded the ship. They looked to discover the cause.

"Hullo! Why, look here! Here we are at Madeira."

They were. So absorbed had they been in conversation as not to notice how near they were to land. The usual excitement of a stoppage now occupied their attention.

The vessel was to stay at Madeira for a time. Stores had to be taken in and the passengers allowed a chance of seeing the place before the vessel was turned for her homeward voyage.

Masters and Dick spent their whole time on shore; always in each other's company. The author explained that he liked sympathy in his admiration for the lions of the port. The one made many sketches and the other many mental notes.

They were quite good friends again.

CHAPTER XXVIII

HOMEWARD BOUND

Two days after; *La Mascotte* steamed away from Madeira. The list of the ship's passengers had been added to. Two new persons were aboard, returning to England.

Masters and Dick were seated on deck in their usual places. The one writing, the other sketching; suddenly a voice behind them said:

"If it were needed, here is more evidence of the smallness of the world."

The voice had that settled Society drawl about it. Particularly unwelcome hearing away from its proper setting: the surroundings in which it is usually to be heard. In its own sphere it is bad enough; is positively jarring in the unconventional atmosphere of aboard-ship life.

At any rate, Dick found it so, if judgment might be framed from his expression. He looked the reverse of pleased, but subdued the feeling as he turned round and spoke:

"Hullo! I didn't see you come aboard. How do you do, old fellow? How do you do, Miss Chantrelle?... Let me introduce Mr. Masters to you." He knew his friend's real name now, and was rather proud of it. "Mr. William Masters.... Yes, the novelist—Miss Chantrelle... Her brother, Percy Chantrelle."

They formed, more or less, a quartette on the voyage home. Dick saw he was in for it and could not help himself—easy-going Dick! Occasionally they paired off: Miss Chantrelle and Dick and the two men.

Masters prided himself on possession of an ability to read faces; he had no liking for the two new ones which had come aboard at Madeira. Miss Chantrelle's more especially repelled him. Not because he preferred her brother; rather that he set up a higher standard as necessary for women than men.

Human nature was a power Masters ever recognized. He could forgive a man being hard, calculating and selfish, but not a woman; in Miss Chantrelle's face he read all those attributes. Still, they were Dick's friends, more or less; so, in a measure, they became his.

Amy Chantrelle was equally quick in facial perusal; speedily read distrust in Masters'. She had not lived in the world without acquiring its knowledge;

was wise enough to appreciate the power in others she possessed herself. She was a distinctly clever, shrewd, woman of the world.

Nothing would have arisen from all this, but for the rattling of Master Dick's tongue. He told of Prince Charlie's matrimonial intent: the possibility of friend merging into brother-in-law. At heart he was so proud of this possibility that he would have liked to proclaim it from the house-tops—masthead would perhaps have been a more suitable word.

Miss Chantrelle listened with interest; scarcely sympathetic interest, but the distinction was not obvious. It was unobserved by Dick, and he felt himself encouraged to expound the subject he had so much at heart. Was led on to so doing by skilfully-put questions such as only a woman would know how to frame.

Amy Chantrelle was greatly displeased; all her sympathy was assumed. The Chantrelles were poor. Both brother and sister were well-favoured; each looked to marriage as a little boat in which the storm of life might be weathered.

They inclined to the belief that Percy was a favourite with Mrs. Seton-Carr. Now that she was a widow there was hope, a very strong hope too, in their hearts that she might be induced to change her name to that of Chantrelle.

As a matter of fact, they were coming to England for the very purpose of trying to induce her to do so; the Seton-Carr bank balance serving as the lodestone.

They had imagined her left fairly well-to-do, but when they saw in the newspapers the amount her husband's estate was sworn under, their breaths were taken away! They promptly packed and set out for England, home and beauty—not forgetting the aforesaid credit balance.

They were greatly disturbed by what they heard on the boat: when Dick told of the position Masters was hoping to fill. The disturbance rapidly shaped into indignation: they looked on it as an endeavour to take the bread from out their mouths. The pleasant voyage they had looked forward to was not without its unpleasant moments.

"Never mind, Percy." The sister speaking to her brother one day. "Given a clear field, you will go in and win yet."

"The clearness of the field is——"

"Leave that to me; I'll make it my business to see that you have a clear field."

The brother shook his head as he responded gloomily:

"Easier said than done, I fancy, Sis. I'm not overbrimming with hope."

"There is no need for despondency. We will arrange to go to Wivernsea right off. That young fool Dick is finger-twistable: I can make him do anything."

The brother needed more than mere words to convince him; observed sneeringly:

"Except propose marriage to you!"

An ugly light came into her eyes. His shaft had gone in up to the feather; she spoke bitterly:

"Yes. He is not of the impressionable kind. I don't suppose any woman will ever get him."

"Odds on that, Amy, if you fail to bring him up to the scratch."

"But I can make him arrange for us to visit there. His sister thinks everything of him.... Masters won't go there."

"Don't be so sure of that."

"I am. He is one of those thin-skinned, sensitive sort of beasts. There has been some misunderstanding—probably of his own creation—which he counts on being able to wipe away. But he has never stayed there; we have. He goes year after year to rooms in the place; he'll put up at the same rooms again."

"Think so?"

"Am certain of it. I can read the man as easily—well, as easily as his books are read."

"Yes, he's read. A popular writer like that must be earning pots of money in royalties. Might be worth setting your cap at, Amy."

He looked at his sister critically. She was a handsome girl. The face a trifle hard, perhaps, but not every man goes in for melting beauty; some look for character—so thought her brother.

Bitter laughter shaped on her lips at her brother's suggestion; a woman ever takes defeat badly; she replied:

"I am not his sort; I am not the kind of woman he writes about! He can dissect me, probably has done so, as easily as you can carve a pigeon. Besides, he's dead gone on Mabel."

"Curse him!"

"By all means. But whatever you do, don't fear him. Outwardly he is as cold as ice; inside there is a raging volcano. Women don't hanker after that kind of love, if there's anything more outwardly tempestuous: like yourself. They are apt to judge of the surface."

"Thanks!"

"Oh! It's true; we don't want to mince words. That's where the average woman makes a fool of herself; where your chance comes in. Masters is worth fifty of you, but there are no scales to balance or register values of that kind."

"Thanks again!"

"Oh, we know it, you and I. We can speak to each other without putting foot on the soft pedal. He has a nature which would make him stick to a woman till, literally, death did them part. Yours is of the type which would prompt thoughts of a separation the moment the woman's bank balance ran out."

"And you?"

He could not resist the sneer; she had fingered a sore place. But he did not hurt her this time; she owned up at once:

"Cast in the same mould! I did not mean blame to you. My own glass-house prevents stone-throwing. I was merely stating facts; I would not have them otherwise. Men like Masters are profitless in this world. When virtue is its own reward, the reward is usually too small to be seen with the naked eye. I have a distinct preference for qualifications which are otherwise."

Percy smiled. Was full of admiration points for his sister. She was the stronger of the two: he ever recognized that; she continued bitterly:

"Virtue is all very well for woman: it may serve her purpose. For a man it is a useless luxury."

His own non-possession of it made him smile again; she went on:

"As you don't seem inclined to take the initiative I shall do so myself. Before we reach Wivernsea, Mabel will have received a letter from me. I am going to write it ready to post at the first port we touch. It will go by the overland route."

It did.

CHAPTER XXIX

ACHING HEARTS AND LAUGHING FACES

The composition of the letter to Wivernsea needed all the powers Miss Chantrelle could bring to bear upon it. They were in no way of a mean order.

She did not, however, grudge time or labour; the expenditure was in a good cause: Percy had been on the matrimonial stocks too long; his was the kind of beauty which age withered rather than ripened.

A little sigh of content escaped her when, at last, she had finished writing. Leaning back in her chair, the end of the penholder between her lips, she read:

> MY DEAREST MAB,—*Isn't* it a tiny little world? Just fancy—my brother and I are coming back to England on the same boat your brother is travelling by! Dear old Dick! He looks so strong and well; better I think than I have *ever* seen him look. With him is Mr. Masters—oh, of course, I ought to congratulate you, oughtn't I?—but I will leave that till I see you. It is a good job you are not of a jealous disposition, Mab, or I am afraid there would be a rough time ahead for you: Mr. Masters is such a *dreadful* flirt! He has been most popular with all the ladies on board, and made *violent* love to me within twenty-four hours of meeting me! He did not succeed in *my* case, though (not because of you, my darling Mab, because I had not heard of your engagement to him then) but I do not like a man who makes love to every woman he meets; whom you run across in odd parts of the boat engrossed in conversation with some pretty girl, generally *a different one each time*. But there, I must not say anything against him, or you will never forgive me. Besides, if you don't mind it, what does it matter? Of course, there's no real harm in what he does—don't think I want to insinuate that, it is the last thing I mean—as the girls must know he is only flirting; perhaps his heart is with you all the time. How beautiful it must be to have such faith as yours—I am afraid I'm not gifted that way. You must be *very* fond of him if all he says is true: that you dote on the ground he walks on, etc., etc., etc. Asked if the marriage day had been fixed, he replied

that that only rested with himself! Fancy that; *Aren't* the men growing dreadfully cheeky? Your brother has asked us to come down to Wivernsea for Christmas. I *never* saw a man grow so awfully white as Percy did when he heard of your forthcoming marriage to Mr. Masters. Till then I had had no idea that he—but there, that would be telling tales out of school. We are coming to spend Christmas, *unless*, dear Mabel, you would rather we did not. If for that or *any reason* you would rather we did not come just now, *wire* to us, care of Charing Cross cloak room, when you get this. *We shall quite understand* that it is not convenient just now. You know what a dear, impulsive boy Dick is; he *absolutely insists* on our coming; says you will be *really* pleased to see us. I do hope so, darling. I have a recollection of many, *many* happy days spent with you.

With *all* my love,
Believe me, *dearest* Mabel,
Your *ever true* friend,
AMY.

As she folded the letter and directed its envelope she muttered:

"I think this puts a spoke in Prince Charlie's wheel! If I know anything of Mabel's pride, this won't ensure open arms and the warmest of welcomes for him."

She hesitated a moment, then laughed; continued:

"There is no scrap of fear of my letter ever being produced. Her pride would not allow her to do that, and she overruns with it."

Amy Chantrelle was a clever woman; that fact has been recorded. In addition to knowing what to say and how to say it, she correctly foresaw just the effect it would produce. Her study of womankind was a very close one.

The letter sent to Wivernsea carried all its intended evil. The descent of a bombshell could not have had a more disturbing effect. After perusal of it, Mrs. Seton-Carr was simply furious. Amy had not relied on the widow's pride in vain. Moreover, her belief in the proverb was justified: throw enough mud, some of it sticks.

The letter was read over and over again. Each time an effort was made to disbelieve its contents, each time the bad impression became deeper: that there is no smoke without fire.

Laughter would have resulted at the impertinence of Masters' conduct, as detailed in the letter, if she had not cared for the man. That was the weak point.

Not a day passed without her thoughts being full of him. The letter came as a blow; a blow of the severely hurting sort. Wounded pride is hard of healing: there is generally some poison in the wound; it is apt to spread too, and endanger the hurt.

By the same mail which brought the Chantrelle episode she received a letter from her brother Dick. It told her that he was coming down to Wivernsea to spend his Christmas; that Prince Charlie was coming too.

Apart from the pleasure of receiving a letter from him written with an unshaking hand and the natural joy she felt at his buoyant style of writing, what he said was a big annoyance to her.

His letter exuded praise of Masters in every sentence. It was easy to read between the lines that he looked upon himself as that gentleman's future brother-in-law. This to Mrs. Seton-Carr could only fit as a confirmation of her friend Amy's letter.

Pride and a readily aroused temper usually battle together with conspicuous success. Mabel worked herself up to such a pitch of excitement that she positively cried. To think that this man—she knew in her heart of hearts that she loved him—should have the effrontery to talk of her so!

Was it to be nothing but insult from him? Could she not—was it not possible to—pay him back somehow? What had she done that he should single her out for annoyance? Whatever it might be, when was she to feel herself free from his cowardly attacks?

If only he were open about the matter; but he was not. Then came remembrance of the time of Gracie's convalescence; how he had ever treated her with uniform courtesy. She remembered, and sighed. The crown of sorrow is the remembrance of happier days.

The inaudible feet of Time continued their never-ending progress. It was not a period in which Mrs. Seton-Carr was at ease; the amount of patience in which she possessed her soul could have been easily balanced on a needle point.

The steamer bringing the quartette reached England. The four passengers kept together; travelled down to Wivernsea in the same carriage. Reached it early in Christmas week.

Dick's reluctance to allow Masters to go to his old lodgings was manifest. There were many spare rooms at Ivy Cottage, he said, so why not go there?

In his opinion it was simply idiotic to pig in at digs. But Masters had ideas of his own; at that moment they did not fit in with his friend's.

The Chantrelles went on with Dick to Ivy Cottage. It was arranged that Masters should turn up there in the evening in time for dinner.

He had been a trifle reluctant to accept that invitation at Dick's hand, but did so. He could have kicked himself, later, for doing so. As for Dick, the nearer they drew to the point where separation must come, the more full of admiration and real affection he became. He rested uneasily whenever his friend was out of his sight.

Masters impatiently ticked off the hours till the arrival of dinner-time. He wanted so to see the woman he loved. Wanted a quiet ten minutes, that he might pour out his heart to her. He was willing to ask her forgiveness on his knees—had she not knelt to him? Had a heart-aching, a tongue-itching, to tell her that she was the one woman in the world for him.

Things are not always disposed as man proposes; he did not tell her that. The quiet ten minutes did not come. When he entered Ivy Cottage before dinner it was with a light heart, the happiest man in Wivernsea. He left it after, with a heart of lead, the most miserable of men.

Beneath the surface, the dinner party was not a success; yet it cannot be said to have flagged. Almost every one was in good spirits, in too good spirits, apparently, to trouble about the quiet man who sat next to Dick.

Dick was thunderstruck at his friend's reticence. Thought at first that he must be, ridiculous as it seemed, suffering from shyness. Mrs. Seton-Carr thought she was getting a little of her own back! She got more; more than all.

Common decency prevented her cutting Masters dead. But, as nearly as was consistent with common politeness, that was what happened. As fuel to fire was the open and violent flirtation of the hostess with Percy Chantrelle.

Exultant as she was of her success, flushed as was her cheek with triumph—she knew Masters was smarting—she feared that she almost overdid it. But the pulsations of Percy's heart were accelerated; beat fast with hope: so did his sister's.

It was impossible to avoid seeing Mrs. Seton-Carr's flushed excitement. Masters noted too the soft glances she shot across the table Percy Chantrelle's way; noticed them with a feeling at his heart which was more than painful.

The author was in possession of more than his usual keenness. Perhaps it out-balanced his power of cool observation. Anyway, he saw not beneath the surface. The soundness of his deductions suffered by reason thereof.

They were happy enough, the brother and sister; the only real happiness there was around the table. Mabel was playing a part: playing it well; wore her mask with success. Her laugh rang out merrily at each of Chantrelle's jokes. But just as full as her face and voice were of mirth, so was her heart full of ache and pain.

Mrs. Seton-Carr would have given worlds just then to be able to rise from her table; she needed so greatly to go to her room for a good cry. But a Lucifer-like pride upheld her. Laugh, and the world laughs with you; weep, and you weep alone. She knew that.

The men did not remain long in union after the retirement of the ladies. To two-thirds of the trinity the cigars seemed flavourless. As a matter of fact, their respective elements lacked the power of combination.

The third factor, Chantrelle, was happy enough; triumph made him so. But there was no infection in his merriment. As a smoking-room raconteur he was usually a big success. But to-night his best stories fizzled out to lame and impotent conclusions.

The laugh of approval was conspicuously absent.

CHAPTER XXX

AS FAITHFUL AS A DOG

The men left the smoke-room; there was no calumet of peace there. All Percy's efforts to be entertaining ended in—perhaps appropriately—smoke. They joined the ladies, to find harmony and concord; music was under way.

Masters was full of thought; deep misery kind. Whatever charm music may have to soothe a savage breast, it had none for him. He was ever a failure at social functions: was conspicuously so to-night; detested them, in fact, with a whole-souled detestation.

As to Dick, the gloom which had fallen on him during dinner seemed too thick for penetration. Merry Dick belied his nickname; had no more merriment in him than has a mute at a funeral.

In the drawing-room Masters was as miserable as he had been in the dining and smokerooms. Turned over photographs; sought in vain for something to make him look less of a fool than he felt. At last came to the end of his endurance tether; under a plea of some work he had to post to a publisher by the early morning's mail, hastily excused himself.

"It's a glorious night, old chap." Dick, speaking hoarsely, and getting into his great-coat. "I'll walk home with you. We will smoke a cigar together."

Masters said good-night; shook hands. Noticed the burning heat of Mrs. Seton-Carr's, as for a moment her hand rested in his—but did not accord the true reason for it. She was even laughing with Chantrelle at the very moment she said good-night; was a natural actress: a woman.

"How quiet Mr. Masters is." The cat purring: Amy speaking, as the door closed. "But I suppose, socially, authors are as dull as ditch water. Keep all their clever thoughts for their books. It is selfish of them in the extreme."

Amy laughed gaily; continued in that strain. Laughter is the allotment of those who win; the Chantrelles felt justified in the belief that they were in no way losing.

Mrs. Seton-Carr professed accord in the opinion of Masters' dulness; the sea voyage had not improved him. Society was not the thing he shone in; in fact, she had found him rather depressing; was glad he left so early. Lies! Lies—each and every one of the opinions she expressed.

The two men who had left the bungalow walked along the Parade for a time without speaking. Each was full of emotion. Dick's found vent first; he blurted out:

"I'm—I'm awfully sorry, old man!"

There was a faint tinge of nervousness in Masters' responding laugh; he was not a man to assimilate pity very well, even his best friends'. Throwing away the cigar, which had gone out, he lighted his pipe; the match betrayed a shaking hand.

"Thanks.... Cloudless night; looks like being a fine day to-morrow, doesn't it?"

The effort to change the subject proved futile; Dick spoke impulsively:

"Hang the weather!... You don't think I knew anything of this, dear old chap——"

"No! No!"

"—or you know I should have——"

"Yes, yes. I know."

"Mab has always professed to positively loathe Percy; tolerated him because she liked his sister. He is a bit of a bounder, you know."

"Your sister does not seem to share in that opinion of yours."

He could not quite keep the bitterness out of the way in which he said that.

"No!"

The brother admitted it; spoke just as bitterly. When they reached his lodgings Masters said:

"Come round, will you?"

"You—you won't come on to the cottage to——"

"Oh, no! No!"

"No. I didn't expect you would. I had counted on things being so different! Counted on a merry Christmas."

Dick laughed as he said, thought of, a merry Christmas: the unpleasant, ironic laugh of a disappointed man. Just then he was as full of disappointment as he could well hold.

"I had gone in for a certain amount of accountancy too."

Masters made the response with a little catch in his voice, which the assumed laugh could not disguise. He had stopped and was standing with his hand on Dick's shoulder.

"Do you remember that last time I held you like this, dear boy? I was so full of joy then, so blinded by it, to what I was doing, that you accused me of squeezing you to hurting point." A sigh punctuated his speech. "I don't feel like hurting you now."

"Squeeze the life out of me, if it will be any relief to your feelings." Dick spoke gruffly. "It's your life. I shouldn't be living at all if it were not for you."

He was a good boy was Dick, with a heart in him; a heart in the right place. It grieved him to see even the suspicion of a tear in the eye of the friend he loved so well.

His own brown eyes looked into the author's with silent, dog-like fidelity and sympathy. Masters was not insensible to it. It was an eloquent silence; expressed far more to him than words could have done.

"I made a mistake, Dick; that's all. I suppose all of us do; the world seems so full of them.... And let this be the last of it, dear old man, will you? Don't recur to it ever again; please. The sore is fresh, and—and—I don't mind owning to you, it hurts. Please don't let us talk about it—ever again— please."

Dick grasped the hand extended to him; held it in a long, tight grip. Put his other hand on his companion's shoulder, and was about to speak. Then felt that speech would be a failure; simply said gruffly:

"I'll see you in the morning, old man; I'll walk round. Good-night."

Not another word passed between them; a tight hand-grip and they parted. Masters to his rooms, Dick homeward bound—a journey he made with the blood coursing through his veins at boiling point. He had more than a little of his sister's temper.

Dick was simply furious at the manner in which Mabel had treated Masters. He dared not trust himself to more talk that night. Just looked into the drawing-room at the bungalow, professed weariness, said a hurried good-night and retired to his room.

In the morning, Gracie offered strong evidence that she had a tongue in her head; was full of the return of Prince Charlie. She had heard of his arrival with delight; was running over with anxiety to see him. Instinctively she felt that Uncle Dick was the ways and means. When she heard that he was going to call on Masters that morning, she emulated the limpet; he could not have shaken her off had he tried.

"Get your things on, Puss," said Dick, as the breakfast things were being cleared away, "and I'll take you round to see him."

Miss Chantrelle professed the most acute astonishment. Not so much by what she said, but the way she acted. Wasn't Mr. Masters coming in to lunch?... Nor to dinner? Not at all that day?... Those carefully combed eyebrows of hers almost disappeared under her fringe—she was so surprised!

Gracie had scampered off and returned in full war-paint: best hat, best shoes, best coat and, crowning glory, new muff! She did hope Prince Charlie would notice it and ask her all about it. But if he did not, she could tell him. That is one of the advantages of being very young.

When Gracie and Dick had gone out, Miss Chantrelle improved the opportunity with her hostess. Nearly drove that lady to the brink of madness by her anxiety to know if they had quarrelled; what it meant; why he wasn't coming, etc.

Mabel did not know; really, the matter was of little interest to her. His presence made very little difference; she wondered Amy could bother about him.

That was what she was able to bring herself to say. But the effort was a big one; she was not a conspicuous success in lies of the top-notch kind.

Matters continued in this way. Things are not always what they seem; it was by no means a pleasant little party at Ivy Cottage. When at home—which was a very rare thing, for he spent most of his time at Masters' lodgings—Dick was sulky to the extreme of sullenness.

Affairs wore a different complexion a little later. When the rosy finger heralded the dawn of the day before Christmas, it was the precursor of brightness of another kind. Two incidents happened which changed the current of things.

Miss Chantrelle had the watchful, veiled eyes of the domestic cat. On the principle of striking the iron whilst hot, she urged her brother to propose marriage to their hostess forthwith. Thought that delays were dangerous.

She took him out for a walk to discuss the pros and cons of the proposal. Was a wise little woman, and a firm believer in the theory that walls have ears. Knowing what she knew, she mapped out the route her brother was to travel in his journey to Mrs. Seton-Carr's heart.

But there is such a thing as being too clever: so sharp that one cuts oneself. The average brain has a direct way of working; sees no by-paths, so wastes no time on them; goes straight to the point.

Amy's cleverness led to her undoing.

CHAPTER XXXI

A TEACUP STORM

The coast being clear, Dick's storm-cloud burst. The Chantrelles out for their walk, he imagined them to be washing their domestic dirty linen, he took the floor.

Being alone, he meant having it out, as he termed it, with his sister. Had quite determined on doing it very quietly and calmly. Whistling a few bars of Rule Britannia by way of appropriate prelude, he said suddenly:

"I am expecting one or two important letters, Mab. I wish directly they come you would send them to the post, will you—re-directed to my club?"

"Re-directed—to—your—club!"

"Yes. I have not quite made up my mind where I shall put up, but I am bound to go into the club each day. You won't forget, will you?"

He made a pretended movement in the direction of the door. She was on her feet in a moment, stopping him; stood by his side in dismay. Seized the lapels of his coat and looked at him reproachfully, horror-stricken; fear for him tearing at her heart-strings.

"Dick!"

"Hullo!"

"What—do—you—mean?"

"What do I me—. Surely I spoke plainly. I just want you to re-direct——"

"Yes, yes, yes. But you are here!"

"Ah! Now. But I am going up to London by the afternoon train."

"To—London!"

"Yes."

Mabel's heart sank. She read obstinacy in that frowning face of his; knew what sort of thing that was to fight; had had experience of it. She played what was usually a trump card.

"And at Christmas time, too! Christmas! You will leave me here alone?"

"Alone? Well—I like that! You have got your dear friends, the Chantrelles. There isn't much of a lonely look about you when Percy is around."

"Dick!"

"Hullo!"

"Don't be horrid!"

"Why? Do you claim a monopoly of the right to be so?"

"Dick!"

Her eyes were flashing now; her face had gone crimson-coloured, and her little foot was tapping the floor. She had emotions which ran up her thermometer with the rapidity of a lightning's flash. The altitude of their tempers just then was about equally high.

"Don't keep calling me Dick like that," he said. "It's irritating."

"What's the matter?"

"With me? Nothing!"

"There is."

"Very well, there is. Have your own way. I know that way—you are like the Pears' Soap boy—you won't be happy till you get it."

"Dick!" She almost spat out his name in her fierce emphasis. "You are not going—you shall not go to town to-day!"

"All being well," he replied calmly—white heat calm—"I shall catch the three-thirty-five up."

She was white too, with annoyance. Managed to choke down some of the things she was burning to say; was alive to what their effect would be if uttered. She knew Dick; experience had taught her how large was the amount of patience needed to cope with his impetuosity. Her foot heavily on the pedal of her temper, she gave forth sweet sounds:

"What does this mean? Tell me, Dick. Why are you going?"

The voice was so very gentle that it hurt Dick to hurt her. But he persisted—the little wretch, to treat his best friend so!—she deserved it. Yawning, he said:

"Oh, I feel like spending a merry Christmas. The kind of thing that clings to Christmas cards and Dickens was so full of, you know. I am afraid there isn't enough merriment to go round here; not enough to satisfy a man with a large appetite for it."

"Why not?"

"Way it is dished up, I suppose: surroundings. I don't like your friends——
"

"My friends!"

The foot slipped off the pedal: the note of temper sounded as she blazed out indignantly:

"Who asked them here?"

Dick shrugged his shoulders. Otherwise disregarded her interruption as he continued:

"—you positively insult mine."

"Insult!"

"I think that's the correct word; I can't find a more expressive one lying about."

"Pray who are the friends of mine that you do not like?"

"Refrain from the obvious! You haven't fifty thousand of them staying in the house just now!"

"The Chantrelles, you mean. I repeat, who invited them here? Answer me!"

She stamped her foot as she let loose her shaft. It went home this time: buried its head, rendering Dick furious. He had cursed himself a hundred times for being the cause of their presence. But for that——

"Look here, Mab, you and I don't want to quarrel."

A quarrel just then was the thing he was itching for; if he could have hit something or somebody it would have been an immense relief to his feelings; he went on:

"I have a friend; a man who saved my life! A man who devoted himself to me; but for whom, I should be now at the bottom of the sea."

"Dick!"

She hid her face in her hands. All the memories she had thrust aside, grateful memories, rushed back on her. She did not want Dick to see what she knew her face would show: horror of her own ingratitude to Masters. The recollection of all he had done for her brother flooded her.

"Oh, it's true! I'm not romancing. When I said good-bye to you in that Lambeth bedroom, I meant it to be a good-bye. I went on board that boat with the full intention of making a hole in the water."

"Dick! Dick! Don't say it!"

"I do say it. I say it emphatically. Life didn't seem worth the living to me. Masters shared my cabin; nursed me; tended me; made me see things differently. In fact, made a man of me. When I think of him, and all he did for me, I cry from my heart: God bless him! God bless him!"

He turned his head that she might not see the tears filling his eyes; continued:

"When I think of the debt I owe him, a debt I would pay with my life cheerfully if it would help him, I—I—I——"

She interrupted him; was standing close to him again, white-faced, dry-eyed, breathing heavily.

"Dick! Dick!" she gasped. "You don't know how you are hurting me!"

"And I bring him here," he spluttered, "to your home. Because it was the only place I could bring him to; because I thought my sister loved me, that she would stretch out a warm hand of welcome to the man who saved me. What happens? What happens? She doesn't throw the plates and dishes at him, but, by God! I wish she had! It would have been better than the cold, cutting, contemptuous nature of her insults!"

He struggled to get free from her arms; they had found their way round his neck, and her head was on his bosom. But she held him too tightly. He was unfair; she knew it; not all the wrong was on her side.

"You think nothing of me, Dick!" Her sobbing expostulation: "You ignore the things he has done; the way he has behaved to me!"

"Yes," replied Dick grimly. "Perhaps it's just as well I do. Gracie tells me that in the dead of night he came, and sat up, and nursed her back to life! That's one of the things he did for you and the child you profess to love so much! He's good at nursing, is Prince Charlie, poor old chap!—I have had some. You have had some. But it seems to have struck us in different lights; to have inspired different feelings. Personally, I'd lay down my life for him! The grandest fellow I ever met; God bless him!"

"Dick! Dick! Dick!"

She covered her face with her hands; the tears were streaming through her fingers. He went on pitilessly; his blood was too hot now for softness.

"You don't see anything to be grateful for in what he did for you. On the contrary, his kindly affection for Gracie is a cause of complaint! You coolly tell me I don't know the things he has done, and how he has behaved to you! 'Prince Charlie'—yes. Gracie was right in naming him so. He is a prince; a Real Prince. The child has more gratitude in her little finger than you——"

She stopped him. Would not let him continue. Placed a hand over his mouth as she cried:

"Dick, you are breaking my heart!"

CHAPTER XXXII

RESUMPTION OF DICK'S GOOD TEMPER

Although she had got her arms round him again, Mabel could not stop Dick's voice. He had something to say and was determined to say it; felt wound up to go.

"Breaking your heart!" he commented contemptuously. "You have already broken his; but you will have Percy to mend yours."

"Percy! How dare you suggest such a thing!"

He looked at her astonished; was startled into absolute amazement at the indignation in her voice as she broke away from him.

"Dare! Well——"

"Percy!" She repeated the name scornfully. "You know I hate, detest, despise, loathe him."

Her face was so very expressive just then that there could be no doubt she was saying what she meant. Dick was quick to realize that. Was so astonished at the turn matters had taken that he could only ejaculate:

"Eh!"

A small word, but all he felt capable of shaping just then; was his way of expressing the unutterable mystification and astonishment which had gripped hold of him.

"You *know* it, Dick!" Boot on floor: tattoo resumed. "Don't stand there with that idiotic vacant look on your face, as if you were surprised to hear it."

Surprised! It was a feeble description; idiotic was distinctly better. He stood as one paralysed, listening whilst she excitedly continued:

"I have told you so dozens, hundreds, thousands, millions of times!"

Trust a woman if she picks up figures to shed them with a lavish hand! The blank look on Dick's face intensified. He shook his head in utter hopelessness; the mystery was too much for him. He was dealing with a woman, and—and—well, he was only an average specimen of a man after all!

"Do I sleep?" He found voice at last; quoted: "Do I dream? Or are visions about?"

"I felt mad when I got the letter to say you insisted on the Chantrelles coming here for Christmas. But I didn't like to disappoint you, Dick, the moment of your home-coming, too."

"I insisted?" He was all eagerness as he blurted out the question. "Who says I insisted?"

"Amy in her letter said so———"

"The awful liar!"

"Nice way to talk of a lady!"

"Lady be—I mean she's not a lady if she set down such a thing in black and white. She so badgered me on the boat with hints for an invitation, that at last, in sheer desperation, I did ask them to come."

"Of course you did! And I wish they were a hundred thousand miles away!"

The blank look of astonishment crept on to his face again as he stuttered:

"You—wish—they———"

"Yes, yes, yes."

"Well, I'm———Do—you—mean—to—tell—me that you weren't glad to see them? When during the whole of the first dinner you did nothing but simper and make eyes and laugh with Percy, till the veriest fool in Christendom could have seen you were head over ears in love with him?"

"I hate him! I hate him! I Hate Him!"

His sister's vehemence partly cleared the clouds away. Acted as a douche on his bad temper, as a tonic to his good one; coolly he said:

"My dear girl, take my advice; you'd better send for the quack! Your mind's unhinged; that's what's the matter with you. You're fairly going dotty! If you hate him, what the dev—deuce did you want to pretend to make love to him for?"

"I d—did it"—she was sobbing in her handkerchief now; all the stiffening gone from her back—"to annoy P—Prince Ch—Ch—Charlie."

What there was left of the look of astonishment quite left his face. The scales fell; his eyes were fully opened. Thrusting his hands into his pockets he said vigorously, characteristically:

"Well—I'm—damned!"

Then hope sprang into his eyes; filled his bosom. There was a tangle somewhere, but he was getting his fingers on the ends: he needed to unravel it. Walking over to, he sat beside his sister, who was sobbing on the sofa.

"Just hold up the water supply, old girl." He spoke with all a brother's brutality. "Turn off the tap, and talk coherently, if it isn't too great a tax. I've only got a man's brain, so you might make an effort and leave off conundruming. The way you women twist up things—well, there! You seem to take a positive delight in making troubles for yourselves and everybody else; put up obstacles and cry because you can't get over them. Why did you want to annoy Masters?"

"He insul—sul—sul—ted me so."

Once more a look of amazement crept on Dick's face as he repeated:

"He—insulted—you—so?"

The idea of Prince Charlie's insulting a woman was—well, he almost laughed as he said:

"For many weeks past he had not seen you; for many weeks past I have been his close companion. During all that time he has spoken of you to me as if you were a goddess, instead of being a little devil with a temper vile enough to provoke a saint. He insult you!"

Then he did laugh—heartily. Began to see that there was a path out of the difficulty—it only needed finding. Let him find it—that was all!

"He c—c—could not have thought m—m—much of me, or he would not have f—f—flirted with every girl on board."

"Flirted! Prince Ch——" His laugh broke out again; into a roar this time. "Why, he was the most taciturn beggar on the boat, to everyone but me! Flirt! That's good. Beyond a 'Good morning,' I never heard him address a woman. If one at table asked him for the water-bottle, he acted as if she had done him a deadly wrong in speaking to him! He was not even on pass-the-salt-and-pepper terms with a lady on board. Flirt! This is really too rich!"

The laughter rang out again. His anger was all gone; his face was all sunshine. There was a comedy side to the affair, after all! That was the side of things Dick was sure to reach sooner or later; his nature tended that way. It served to detect the merest trace of humour in things.

"Dick!"

A misgiving was seizing her. She was putting two and two together and making a decidedly unpleasant four of it; said:

"Isn't it true that he made violent love to Amy directly she came on board?"

"To Amy! To Amy! If there was one woman he avoided—positively avoided—more than another, it was Amy. He seemed to take a dislike to her directly she was introduced; and in justice to her, I am bound to say that she reciprocated. From her point of view, I suppose that was showing proper feeling. She was for ever trying to poison my mind against him. But I knew him, and I knew her. She preached to the winds!"

Dick had to pause. Having got hold of the offending root, his indignation was rising, getting the better of him.

"Make love to her!" he repeated. "Good Heavens! Beyond 'Good morning' and 'Good night' I don't suppose he spoke a hundred words to her on the whole voyage home."

"Then—I—I—have been made a fool——"

"Rather an easy task, I should imagine," interjected Dick, with truly brotherly contempt. "But who is responsible for the job? Whoever it was, couldn't have been killed with the hard work!"

"Wait."

She ran out of the room to her bedroom. Quickly opening a drawer, made a moment's search therein. Then returned with a letter in her hand—triumphant.

"It is not altogether correct form for a woman to show a man another woman's letter, but read that."

Dick sat down at the table and she smoothed the document out before him with a degree of gusto. It was her warrant of justification; the only title-deed she possessed to the behaviour of which she had been guilty.

He read it. His face became worth watching as he did so. Amusement, loathing, astonishment, all held sway on it at odd times. Despite his disgust though, there was big hope in the sediment. As he concluded he whistled his favourite "Rule Britannia."

"Well?"

She had been eagerly watching him. Read the answer in his face, but woman-like asked what she already knew:

"Isn't it true?"

"True!" He tossed the letter back to her as he answered. "From beginning to end it is a tissue of deliberate lies."

She heard rapturously. The moral worth of her friend Amy and the ultimate destination of Amy's soul, were matters for future commiseration. They sank into insignificance before the resuscitation of her faith in Masters. That mighty edifice had been obscured by clouds; the clouds were clearing and the proud summit was peeping through.

So glad was she, that she positively revelled in the admission of her own gullibility; said joyously:

"Lies! And I believed them!"

"That doesn't astonish me! I used to think you were a sensible girl, but now—well, there! But there's more than mere lies in that letter."

"What?"

"You can't see it? And you think yourself cute! Can't you read between the lines?"

"What?"

"I told Amy of Prince Charlie's love for you; that started the ball. What does she set herself to do? Poison your mind against him. Why? Note the lie about Percy's turning white when——Good Lord, you can see through it now, can't you? You don't want spectacles for that? Your own common sense will tell you—though you certainly don't seem to have a large supply on hand."

"I—she wanted me—wanted her brother to——"

"That's it! You've got the hammer on the nail head at last! That accounts for her questioning me as to how you were left under the will; whether the money was settled on you or not."

"What a perfect pair of beasts!"

"Hear, hear!"

"And you invited them here! How could you? They are not fit people to have in the house!"

"I like that! Upon my word! See how gone you were on Percy at din——"

"Dick! If you ever dare to say——"

"Well, I must see about packing up——"

"Packing up! Don't let me think you quite a complete idiot, Dick!"

"The train goes at three-thir——"

"Dick!" She stamped her foot in anger. "Why do you want to make it worse for me than it need be by your stupidity. You perfect horror, you!"

"Stupidity runs in the family, I suppose. You have been mighty wise, haven't you? Um—you don't want me to go, then?"

"And leave me in this hopeless muddle alone? It wouldn't be commonly human—to say nothing of brotherly!"

"Oh, well." He affected a resigned air to hide his smiles. "I suppose I'll have to stop if you put it like that. I'll just walk up to Prince Charlie's place and tell him I shan't be able to go up with him."

"To—go—up—with—him?"

Dismay caused her to voice the question in instalments. Dick stooped, pretended to tie up his shoe-lace, some act was necessary to hide from her the amused look in his eyes.

"Yes. I'd like to say good-bye to the dear old chap. He'll probably go abroad and stop there. Maybe I shall never see him again."

"Abroad! Never—see——"

Then she stopped dead in the middle of what she was saying; stood as one dumbfounded. Dick's eyes in his averted head were twinkling and his mouth twitching. She certainly had some ground for the opinion she expressed of him.

He was a brute of a brother.

CHAPTER XXXIII

A TANGLED TRINITY

An observer might have imagined Dick possessed of a just grievance against his tailor; it took him such a while to get into his coat. He was doing so to the accompaniment of "Rule, Britannia," pursed-up lips fashioning it. The difficulty with his coat was one of his own creation; he was thoroughly enjoying the situation and prolonging it as long as possible. The whistling served as a sort of slow music to his little drama.

There was not even a whisper of Masters' leaving England. Indeed, it was pretty certain that had he been going abroad, Dick would have been on hand as his travelling companion. He was, as he termed it, rubbing it in. Brothers are awful brutes at times.

"Dick! Dear Dick!"

She had come to him affectionately; had put her arms round his neck.

"Hold on there! Don't go slobbering on my front again; it is all limp and wet now. I don't want to get inflammation of the lungs through wearing a damp shirt! You are too liberal with your grief, Sis; keep some of it for your handkerchief."

"I'm not crying. Dick—Dick—dear, dear old Dick." She was whispering in his ear in an artful way that she had never known him able to resist. "You know you would not like to make me miserable—your own loving sister——"

He was grinning from ear to ear. The humour of the situation appealed to him as he interrupted:

"None of your blarney; none of your soft sawder! What's the meaning of this sudden overflowing, spring-up-in-a-moment affection? I was an idiot, fool, stupid, a few minutes ago."

"Dear Dick!"

"Yes, that's all very well. But what is it? This sudden discovery of my value means you want something."

She put her mouth close to his ear and whispered again. A very low whisper; he only just caught it:

"Don't let him go, Dick."

"Let who go?"

She knew that to be an evasion; that he was wilfully misunderstanding her. Just shook him and whispered earnestly:

"Please!"

Dick was magnanimous; he could afford to be. His deep-laid scheme had proved successful.

"Well, I'll see what I can do. But what are you going to do about the Chantrelles?"

A change came over her face; every scrap of softness seemed to fade out of it. In a voice full of determination she said:

"The Chantrelles will leave here before the day is over!"

"Rule, Britannia" once more thrilled the air as the whistler caught his sister in his arms.

"You're a brick, old girl." He kissed her. "Things will pan out all right after all. Now, shall I stay and bear a hand, or would you rather handle the precious couple all by yourself?"

There was a steely glitter in her eye—it boded ill for the absent ones—as she answered vindictively:

"I think I can manage alone!"

"I think you can, old girl!... Do you know," he added with mock severity, "when you look a little demon like that, I don't somehow fancy trusting my friend into your keeping. One good turn——; you know the rest. I believe I should be carrying that out by preventing his marrying you."

"He hasn't asked me yet!"

She spoke saucily with sparkling eyes; yet with a rosy blush on her face.

"That's true; perhaps he won't! There's hope for the poor beggar after all! He came all the way from the Mediterranean framing words how he should ask you to marry him, and he had a narrow escape on the dinner party night. Perhaps you killed him then by your nice behaviour; killed any desire he might have had to marry you." Then he added maliciously: "Let's hope so, for his sake."

"Dick! You are a perfect horror!"

"It was 'Dear Dick' a minute ago! But there—you're as uncertain as the weather."

The shot went home; told in the flushed, shamefaced look; Dick inquired:

"What are you going to say to the Chantrelles?"

"That is my business. They will travel up by the afternoon train. Your business is to go to Prince Charlie, and see that he comes here to-night to dinner."

He sobered down in a moment at that; answered seriously:

"No, old girl, that is out of the question. Nothing I could say would induce him to that. He simply hates the Chantrelles."

"I have told you—they won't be here."

"Even the knowledge of their absence wouldn't make him come to your house, after the way in which you behaved to him last time."

"All the same," she said defiantly, "a place shall be set for him at table."

"Look here, old girl, I'm willing to help you, but don't make a pocket idiot of yourself. I tell you nothing I could say would induce him to——"

"Well, you can get him to go for a walk, I suppose, can't you?"

"You know we always go for a walk late every afternoon—weather permitting or otherwise."

"Very well; this afternoon walk eastwards. You know the seat at the end of the Parade?"

"You mean, that one by the wall, which Gracie calls Our Seat?"

"Yes. Make your way there; walk to that, sit down and wait—till I come."

It dawned on him then: her intent. Admiration of her diplomacy found vent in the strains of "Rule, Britannia."

"Don't say anything, Dick. Promise me that. Not a word to Prince Charlie about—about—anything."

"But when you turn up at the seat, what am I to do? I suppose it will be a case of two's company, three's none?"

"Oh, you can go and pick shells and seaweed on the beach!"

"What! In the dark? Is thy brother a dog that he should do these things? I'll find my way back by myself. You think he'll see you home?"

"You can rely on it he will."

Mrs. Seton-Carr had confidence in herself. Perhaps it was as well; few things are won without that.

"All right. We shall be there about five o'clock."

"So shall I."

"Right.... There are the Chantrelles coming up the road; I'll clear out the back way. If they are going, I'd rather be spared saying farewells. I might introduce some choice expressions of my opinion of them."

"Leave that to me!"

Mabel spoke with bitter sweetness. One glance at her face convinced Dick that he could do so with safety.

"Right!"

He disappeared through the back as the Chantrelles entered by the front door. Mrs. Seton-Carr was waiting for them. She smiled pleasantly, iced pleasantry, and invited them into the drawing-room. Seated, she faced them. There, wasted no time in preliminaries; struck out:

"There is something I want to clear up, Mr. Chantrelle."

She fixed that gentleman with her eyes. On her face was a pleasant smile; it never faded once during the interview.

"Yes?"

"About Mr. Masters," she continued. "There has been something unpleasant—so far as he is concerned—said of the voyage home you all made from the Mediterranean. Did you ever see him attempt to make love to your sister?"

"Great Scott! No. He seemed to like her about as little as Amy liked him."

From the corner of her eye, Mrs. Seton-Carr could see that her dear friend Amy had grown very white—Amy had a quicker brain than had her brother—but she never lost her hold on Percy's face; went on:

"Did he bear the reputation of a lady-killer? Of making love to every woman on board?"

"My dear Mrs. Carr!" Percy laughed heartily as he replied, "I never saw him talk to a woman! He had the reputation on board of being a woman-hater. He was a perfect bear!"

Amy glanced at her brother reproachfully, meaningly—too late. Besides, he was looking at his hostess and not at her; her telegraphic communication was without effect. It was a pity, a thousand pities, from Amy's point of view. She had to sit quiet and listen.

"Thanks so much," Mrs. Seton-Carr was saying sweetly. "You see, I was told all that, and it was not a pleasant thing to be told. You must understand that I am engaged to be married to Mr. Masters shortly—but I think you knew that?"

Percy's face fell; all the merriment dropped out of it. A moment's silence ensued; not what could fairly be labelled a dull moment. Then Percy broke it; said slowly:

"No; I had not the slightest idea of such a thing."

"Is that possible? Surely your sister told you! She says in this letter that when you heard of my forthcoming marriage to Mr. Masters you grew white. Although why," she laughed, "you should grow white, I cannot conceive. Our pleasant intercourse has always been quite platonic, hasn't it? That was its charm; one has so few friends. You know that?"

"I—yes. Now I know it."

"I am sorry to say it, Mr. Chantrelle, to you; you always have behaved as a gentleman to me; but this letter," she held it out to him, "written by your sister whilst on the boat, is a tissue of lies from beginning to end. The work of a woman absolutely unfitted—in my opinion—for decent society!"

Brother and sister were on their feet in a moment. The atmosphere seemed red-hot to them. They had had unpleasant moments in their somewhat adventurous career, but this was the worst. Their hostess's words were as the lashes of a whip.

Chantrelle muttered something about breaking the laws of hospitality; a weak effort to stand up for his sister. It failed half-way. Then he abandoned her to her fate.

"Take me away, Percy," his sister gasped. "I will not stay to be further insulted."

"Miss Chantrelle has forestalled me." Mrs. Seton-Carr still spoke quietly, still retained her seat. "That is precisely what I was about to ask you to do, Mr. Chantrelle. One can lock up from a thief, but a liar—a deliberate, scheming, unscrupulous liar—there is no guarding against. Your sister, by her trickery, came near separating me from the man who loves me, the man I love. I should not forgive it in fifty lifetimes."

Miss Chantrelle made an effort to speak. Her lips moved, but for once in her life she was unable to fashion words. She was a woman who trusted to a well-oiled tongue for squeezing out of the tightest places. It failed her now; the effort ended in a gasp.

"Go and pack your things, Amy."

Her brother spoke sternly. The white-faced woman almost staggered out of the room without a word. She was terribly upset; none of us like to be found out in our little lapses.

"Read the letter, Mr. Chantrelle; I request you to. It will convince you that I am not more than necessarily bitter——"

"There is no need. Your word is sufficient."

Mr. Chantrelle bowed; had changed his tactics and was making the best of his position. His sister had led him into this; he would stand by her up to a point, but at the same time he would do what he could to save his own skin. There was no sense in needless sacrifice.

"I know you well enough, know you could only behave as you are doing with good reason," he continued. "I am heartily sorry. Amy is my sister; I am bound to remember that whatever she has done." He held out his hand. "Good-bye. I can only ask you to acquit me personally of any—but there; explanations are perhaps better left alone. Good-bye—it will be well for us not to meet again."

A note of feeling vibrated in his voice. A mere listener to the actual words would have detected no false ring in them. Would, perhaps, have admired him for the staunchness he exhibited towards his misguided sister.

But his hostess stood face to face with him, and she saw that in his eye— lack of sincerity—which discounted the ingenuousness of his speech. Still Mrs. Seton-Carr agreed with it—in substance.

"Good-bye. Yes, it is certainly better so.... My maid shall go across to the station for a porter and truck. They will be here by the time you have packed."

They were. The Chantrelles left. Journeyed to London by the train Dick had mentioned; the most crestfallen couple travelling in it.

It was the last of them.

CHAPTER XXXIV

OUR SEAT

The Chantrelles gone, with the whistle of their departing train shrilling in her ears, Mabel sighed contentedly, gathered all there was of her together and spent a full two minutes in inspecting its reflection in the mirror.

The sound of the closing of the door on them as they left had been sweet music in her ears. The warning shriek of the engine as it started out of the station, drawing them every moment further and further away from her, was sweeter still.

Then she entered into consultation with her cook; set about ordering the most appetising little dinner she could devise. There was entailed an expenditure of anxious thought; the function was an important one. Mrs. Seton-Carr was not a woman to despise details of that kind.

She had laughed once at a cynic's belief that, if you cannot make sure of retaining a man's love, you can, by securing the services of a good cook, make sure of his respect. Despite her laughter she was not without faith in the proverb that the road to a man's heart lies through his stomach.

The last time Prince Charlie had dined at Ivy Cottage he had not enjoyed himself; she remembered why with a little flush of shame. There was determination that he should do so this time. And she rather thought she would enjoy herself too; anyway, it would not be her fault if they failed to do so.

The shades of evening began their descent soon after half-past four o'clock. It was not too dark then for her to see her brother and Prince Charlie go by on the Parade—eastwards. The author's broad, square shoulders were unmistakable. She herself was hidden by the bedroom curtain she was behind.

They had gone in the direction of the seat. A smile found place on her face; so far all was well. Then she tried on two or three hats. Was anxious to look her best; she knew that she could talk so much better when sure of her appearance. Sadness tinged her reflection; the beauty of her millinery would be wasted in the darkness.

Then, with a sigh—she was a woman, with all a woman's belief in millinery's power—she hoped that not much talking would be needed. Silence and a good profile were more reliable. She looked at the clock: the minutes dragged slowly.

At a quarter to five she left the cottage. Before the hour reached the end of the Parade. An east wind was blowing. As she neared the seat the odour of cigars came to her, borne on the wind from which the smokers were sheltered. Then she advanced.

"Hullo, Sis!"

Dick started to his feet as if she were an apparition, spoke in an exaggerated tone of surprise; continuing:

"Who on earth would have thought of seeing you here?"

She could have soundly boxed his ears for him—well-meaning Dick—for so overdoing it. He could not have exhibited more surprise had he thought her dropped from the clouds. Brothers really are terribly trying at times.

Perhaps it was as well for him that he slowly moved away. Apparently he evinced a judicious, if sudden, interest in moonlight conchology. Anyway, he devoted his attention to some of the common objects of the sea-shore.

That Dick did move off was the essential point. She saw, with relief, that he had sense enough for that. The sound of the whistling of "Rule Britannia" gradually died away in the distance.

Masters had risen to his feet the moment his eyes fell on her. Stood there doubtful what he should do. She did not leave him in doubt long; advanced towards him, and stretching out her hand, said:

"Prince Charlie, I am—oh, I am so sorry! Please forgive me!"

It was a lame speech. She was surprised at, ashamed of, herself. She had rehearsed what she had intended saying all the afternoon. Now it came to the point she could not remember a word.

Whatever she might think of her own words they were an immense surprise to Masters. He took her extended hand, common courtesy compelled him to that, and said gently:

"Forgive? You are surely—oh, I have nothing to forgive!"

"You have!"

She insisted with a charming insistence. Somehow her eyes got to need mopping with her handkerchief—a lace handkerchief with a singularly pretty border, by the way.

"I have b-behaved"—she mopped on—"like a wicked wretch t-to you."

Of course, with a man of Masters' temperament it was most effective; she was playing an ideal game. Some men are used to tears; come to look upon them as an unavoidable factor in their dealings with women. The author had not reached that stage: probably never would.

A woman crying, or in distress, never failed to appeal to him. Perhaps Mrs. Seton-Carr knew that. Women are very subtle; their intuition is no mythical possession. Any way, she played that handkerchief of hers for all it was worth.

Masters still stood hesitating; was genuinely anxious and full of wonder: what he ought to do. Thoughts of eau de Cologne occurred to him. He knew women found relief in that kind of thing; but he bent over her and said:

"I beg you—oh, I beg, earnestly, you will not distress yourself."

He really meant it; her distress distressed him. The more she saw that the more tears she shed. Artful little crocodile!

"You w-won't f-f-forgive me!"

She knew all the time that he would.

"Pray, Mrs.—you—I—I—have nothing to forgive. But if you think I have, I forgive you freely, fully."

The road was getting smooth, she thought, but it was not safe to drop the handkerchief yet; plainly that was a strong weapon.

"You m-m-must think me such an awful b-b-brute!"

Wretched little prevaricator! She knew quite well that he thought nothing of the kind.

"Believe me, I can never think of you in any way but the kindliest."

True; every word of it. His heart was like a photographic plate, capable only of bearing one clear picture.

"I d-daresay you wish me dead, or at the bottom of the s-sea—and I d-deserve it."

Really she did. It was most unfair—this present performance of hers. It distressed him beyond measure; he said:

"I wish you nothing but the greatest happiness it is possible for you to enjoy; wish it from my heart."

"And I—I—have behaved so—s-s-so ungratefully to you."

She uttered truth; perhaps for a change. But he denied what she said; answered:

"Not at all! You behaved rightly; as your heart dictated."

She had to flare up at that; could not help it. As a matter of fact all her actions had been in direct opposition to her heart's promptings.

"I did nothing of the sort! My behaviour was quite wrong!"

The handkerchief shifted a little to enable her to look up at him out of the corner of her eye, as she continued:

"Just the reverse of the way my h-h-heart dictated."

His own heart beat a little quicker at that, in expectation, as he asked eagerly:

"When was that?"

"At that wr-r-retched dinner."

He sat down; somehow they both sat—apparently it was a simultaneous act. He was, however, to windward of her; she engineered that. The faint perfume of the hair of her bent head came to him. It has been already mentioned that Mrs. Seton-Carr devoted attention to details. No wonder the elder Weller warned his son against widows!

"You have said either not enough or too much." He spoke hoarsely, in tense tones. "Tell me—more."

"You want to make it h-h-hard for me; to humble me m-m-more."

She sobbed out the words, the while her disengaged hand, curiously, fell on his. Naturally, his hand closed on hers, and—quite easily—he frustrated her efforts to take it away. He moved closer to her.

She turned the back of her head to him. Was not unaware of the fact that her hair grew very prettily there; fell in soft little golden curls at the nape of her neck. Of course the movement was quite an unconscious one! Perhaps, too, it was pure accident that the moon just then had popped from behind a cloud, so lighting up things; she went on:

"I t-think you are very h-hard to me."

He moved closer still; every fibre in his being thrilled by contact with the woman he loved. Had he bent down, his lips would have touched her head. The blood was racing through his veins as he wondered—should he dare? Then he thought of the dinner party—remembered Chantrelle. The thought acted as the descent of iced water might have done: she was another man's property! He took his hand away.

That alarmed her—dreadfully! She had thought all was going along so nicely; was actually getting ready for the union of lips; the final drying of her eyes. What could possibly have frozen him up like that?

"I am sorry," he said, "you should think unpleasant things of me. But is there need?"

The coldness of his tone struck a horrible chill to her heart. But it was not a moment for despair, rather for a marshalling of all her forces. She redoubled her efforts; fell on her knees by his side, and cried:

"You are cruel! I am kneeling to you, asking you to forgive me, and you won't! I knelt to you once before—here on this spot—and you were cruel to me then——"

"Ah, yes!"

He interrupted her; the memory of his brutality then—he called it so—returned to him; his words came hurriedly:

"For that I need your forgiveness; I ought to abjectly apologise. What I did, said, then was wholly under a misapprehension——"

She seized on that: it gave her a chance. Moreover, it was now or never—so she thought. Metaphorically she set her teeth and said—Now. Actually she whispered:

"Isn't it possible perhaps, that you may be under a misapprehension now?"

She boldly raised her head and looked him straight in the face as she spoke. Tears had not in the least, strange to say, disfigured hers; her grief had not been that kind! She continued:

"Don't do as you did then; don't push me away from you!"

That was a rubbing of it in with a vengeance. Had the effect of making him speak with a strange quiver in his voice.

"Please—please get up! I don't like—I can't bear—to see you——"

Her disobedience was of the studied kind. She got so close to him that he felt the warmth of her body, the up-creep of her hands on his breast, the sweet warm breath from her lips. So holding him—holding in every sense of the word—she said with a spice of defiance in her voice:

"I won't get up till you tell me you forgive me everything!"

She had him at such a disadvantage! It was really grossly unfair. The poor wretch did not know whether he was on his head or his heels. Then, almost before he knew what he was doing, his arms were about her; he could not help it. He gripped her to him so closely that she could have cried out—but it was too sweet a pain to ask relief from.

"Tell me." His voice was raucous in its hoarseness. "You do not—do not belong to Chantrelle?"

A laugh came to her lips. A tinge of jealousy in the man she loves pleases a woman, spices things as it were. Besides, looked at from the right viewpoint, it is the subtlest of flattery.

Hence her laughter.

CHAPTER XXXV

CHRISTMAS EVE

Mrs. Seton Carr seemed in no hurry to withdraw herself from the author's tightly clasping arms. Seriously, it was really very disgraceful behaviour of hers. She excused herself with the knowledge that there was no audience: save the moon and the sea. After subsidence of her laugh she said:

"I have said good-bye for ever to the Chantrelles. They have left Ivy Cottage. I shall never see them again———"

"I thought———"

"I loved him?" she interrupted gleefully. "I didn't—I just hated him———"

"Yet you———"

"Pretended I did because I wanted to annoy you! There! I wanted to annoy you because—I.... Don't, Prince Charlie! You're making me look so untidy.... Yes do—I don't mind.... They'll think it was the wind."

Thoughts of other people and of dinner came to them at last. But it was half-past seven before they started to walk back home. What they said during all the time they were on the seat is a matter of concern to themselves only.

Besides which, when people are in love, their conversation is not remarkable for originality and general interest. Even authors get out of the stirrups—off their high horse—and talk like other people.

She explained to him that she had loved him from the first. He, wondering how he could have been blind to the fact, hugged her close again. Thereupon, she complained that he hurt her, and then contradicted herself; in fact behaved like a true woman.

She confessed why she had not told him she was Mrs. Seton-Carr at first: because she was a leader of London fashion, and she knew he hated London Society and everything connected therewith. The newspaper people chronicled her movements and she was much talked about; she had thought he would not fail to recognize her name.

But she need not have feared; he would not have done so. Fashionable Intelligence, and all columns captioned in kindred fashion, he never read. Had an idea of his own that in the study of mankind his society papers were not very suitable textbooks.

It would naturally be supposed that seeing how late it was they would have hurried home. Not they! It was nearly eight o'clock when they reached Ivy Cottage. Dick was waiting for them.

"This is a pretty idea, upon my soul!" His greeting. "A nice way to treat your brother! Dinner has been waiting hours!"

"Never mind, Dick dear," replied his sister, pecking at his lips as she removed the pins from her hat. "It doesn't matter, it really doesn't matter in the least."

"Doesn't it! It matters to me! Am I supposed to be a fasting man, giving a seaside exhibition of myself? There's been no midday meal, because I had to bolt whilst you were turning people out of the house neck and crop. I did think I was going to get some dinner! I don't even get an apology. You're flouncing around grinning all over your face as if you'd picked up sixpence. What have you been doing?"

"There—sit down—like a good boy. Here's the soup coming. Now start and try to make up for lost time."

She ran to her room and threw off her hat and mantle. Laughed at her reflection in the glass—a laugh inspired by sheer happiness. Then she crept softly into Gracie's room; the child was not yet asleep, though sleepy. Bending over the cot she kissed the little rosy face, and Gracie's arms went up and around the neck of her Dear Miss Mivvins.

Mrs. Seton-Carr had not been away from the dining room more than two minutes; when she returned to take her place at table mischievous Dick was ready waiting for her, said:

"What I want to know is, what the deuce you two have been sitting out on that blessed seat all night for? Why couldn't you come in like rational beings and sit in chairs and talk?"

"Never you mind, Dick; don't ask questions. Have some more soup?"

"Oh, you can't stop my mouth with soup! I have been kept without food for so long that I'm afraid to eat much! I expect it was some of that tommy-rot Prince Charlie was always flooding my ears with. About your eyes and hair and——"

"Now, Dick," interrupted Masters, "drop that please. It is a forbidden subject."

"Is it? I am not to talk about what you said?" He turned to his sister and continued: "What have you had to say then, Sis? Been telling him how you begged and prayed of me not to let him——"

"Dick! If you don't be quiet, I'll never forgive you!"

"Now, look here." Dick assumed an aggrieved tone. "Am I supposed not to talk at all? Is this house run on the silent system? I might just as well be having dinner in a deaf and dumb asylum."

"Talk sensibly then," said his sister patronisingly, "and we'll listen to you with pleasure."

"We! Oh, it's reached that stage, has it: plural! 'M very well. Let's take up a serious subject: horribly serious. Have you lunatics decided when your two throbbing hearts are going to be merged into one; when you are to be married?"

"Dick! Don't you want—let me pass you some more vegetables!"

"Don't stop his thirst for information," interposed Masters quietly. "He's got to be best man, so he may as well know. It is settled that we are to be married by special licence on New Year's Day."

"Oh, Prince Charlie!" she cried. "I never said—indeed I didn't——"

"No, dear," he replied calmly. "I know you did not. But you said that that woman I made love to on the boat—what was her name?—Amy—pass the sauce, Dick—alleged that I said it rested with me, so far as the naming of the day was concerned."

"How can you——"

"It occurred to me that that was a capital idea. I am not one of those superior persons; am never above taking a hint. I know I have had—thanks to you—the most unhappy end of a year. By way of compensation I am going—thanks to you again—to have a most happy beginning of one."

Dick viewed the consternation displayed on his sister's face to the accompaniment of a broad grin on his own, said:

"That's right! Start quarrelling now, even before you are tied up! Goodness knows what it will be like after, when you are sentenced to—I mean when you are linked for life. Miserable wretches! You have my sincerest sympathy; all my pity."

"It takes two to make a quarrel."

Prince Charlie uttering the aphorism. Then with a smile, holding out his hand to Mabel, he continued:

"You agree with me, don't you, darling? Just by your action convince this beardless youth that we are in accord about the first of January—if we are to be married on that day, put your hand in mine."

She hesitated a moment, perhaps her brother's derisive laugh helped to her action: she put it right there.

"There's one thing about this affair—having long been an acute sufferer from my headstrong sister's temper," said Dick, grinning all over his face— "about which I am distinctly displeased."

"You are going to make one of your terrible jokes, Dick!" she said. "I can see it in your face!"

"Oh, let him run loose," interposed Masters. "It's Christmas time, you know. What's the joke? If it's going to give us pain, out with it—as the boy said to the dentist."

"If you labour over one of your usual atrocious puns, Dick," warned his sister, "I'll throw you down and pummel you black and blue!"

"I was merely going to observe," said her brother, regardless of the threat, "that I was glad that at length you had found your master!"

He had to howl for mercy before she let him go.

CHAPTER XXXVI

THE CHRISTMAS BOX

Gracie had to be reckoned with. Prince Charlie was looked on as her exclusive property. Considerable diplomacy and tact would have to be brought to bear; that exacting atom of humanity needed careful handling.

Uncle Dick, with a thoughtfulness which earned from his sister and prospective brother-in-law grateful thanks, went out, late as it was, and routed round the few shops of which Wivernsea boasted. The shops were full of people and empty of wares. By diligent search he ran to earth in a grocer's shop a box of crackers, packed by Tom Smith, as he needed to find it packed: labelled Pantomime. He thought that would answer the purpose of conciliating his niece.

He was not disappointed. On the morrow, with a harlequin's cap and mask, a wand, and conjured up recollections of last year's pantomime all went well. Promise of a visit that week to another pantomime completed the matter. There was no breach.

Gracie gave up all rights in Prince Charlie. Indeed, viewed his changing into the character of a new papa with curious equanimity. Curious, that is to say, to any one ignorant of her knowledge of the doings of fairies. The literature upon which she fed was of the divided syllable type. A story without a fairy in it was beneath her contempt.

So it was that on Christmas morning she viewed the matter complacently. Having disposed of Prince Charlie to her mother, she gave him Miss Mivvins as a Christmas box. Borrowed his fountain pen, and in a large round hand wrote:

"*With best wishes for a Merry Christmas and a Happy New Year.*"

Dancing up to, and putting this into Miss Mivvins' hand, she gracefully led that lady to her former prince; was rejoiced when she saw how glad he was to accept her gift!

And the wish was realized too: their Christmas was of the merriest. Gracie said she had never spent so happy a one in all the years of her life; was of opinion that the harlequin had been at work with Uncle Dick; he was so different from what he used to be.

Uncle Dick was, and he knew it. Looked back at his past with eyes full of horror, at his prospective brother-in-law with love in them, because he felt, knew, to whom his reformation was due.

Gracie's other wish was granted: the new year was a happy one. It commenced with the actual transformation of Prince Charlie into Gracie's new papa. The child said she had never made a change which pleased her so much.

As Gracie wisely observed, it was not now a matter of occasional calls, he was always there. So much better, wasn't it? She really thought they had all been quite foolish not to think of arranging it so before.

As to Uncle Dick—well, as Gracie said, he was changed. And it was a permanent change, too; he feared no relapse. Just sometimes the memory of the old evil times would return, and a suspicious moisture come into his eyes. He could not help thinking of what might have been, and what was. Thanked God from his heart for his present condition.

As to Miss Mivvins—well, of course she no longer exists. She merged into Mrs. Masters on the first day of the new year.

Another change which had Gracie's full approval.

THE END.

Milton Keynes UK
Ingram Content Group UK Ltd.
UKHW030719041024
449263UK00004B/384

9 789362 098757